An Irish Tragedy

An IRISH TRAGEDY

HOW SEX ABUSE BY IRISH PRIESTS HELPED CRIPPLE THE CATHOLIC CHURCH

JOE RIGERT

CROSSLAND PRESS
2008

Published in the United States by
Crossland Press
P.O. Box 26290
Baltimore, MD 21210

ISBN-13: 978-0-9790279-8-7
ISBN-10: 0-9790279-8-5

Printed in the United States of America

Contents

Introduction

"OH, THE POOR IRISH," exclaimed Tony Flannery when I explained the purpose of my visit—to examine the scandal of clergy sex abuse in his country. Indeed, the Irish have suffered much: oppressed for generations under English rule, once decimated by famine, mired in the mud of poverty, victimized by prejudice as migrants to America. And now, shamed by the pervasive sexual abuses of their priests. Despite this history, Flannery was not defensive. As a leading critic and reformer in the Irish Catholic Church, a role that has cost him any prospects of career advancement, Flannery knows that healing can only come through addressing the church's problems openly and frankly.[1]

My goal in traveling to Ireland was to get insights from people like Flannery on the causes and extent of sexual abuse in that country, and to determine to what extent Irish priests had contributed to the monstrous sex-scandal in the American church.

I didn't set out to write a book on Irish priests. Rather, I started my journey with a broad inquiry into the sexual involvements of Catholic bishops in North America and Europe. Upon retiring after 40 years in print journalism, I was struck by how the American priests were taking so much of the blame for the sex-abuse problem, while their superiors, the bishops, remained above it all. I had personal, as well as professional, reasons for pursuing the truth. My brother Jim, a priest and now-retired faculty member at the University of Notre Dame, told me how he felt under suspicion whenever he appeared publicly in priestly garb, as though he were one of the evil abusers. As for me, the scandal added to my doubts about the church that helped nurture and educate me. With my own genetic and journalistic distrust of power and authority, I wondered how many of the bishops had been involved in sex abuse and how they had avoided scrutiny.

Here was an opportunity to produce an epic story on one of the greatest scandals in the history of the Roman Catholic Church, rivaling the mere sale of tickets to heaven, which had led to the Protestant Reformation. How would the historians look upon this in the year 3,000? I would try to describe it here and now. Thus began my laborious task of collecting the names of every bishop publicly accused of sexual abuse, and then going from courthouse to courthouse in the United States and Canada, from Florida to California and British Columbia, reading every document on every errant bishop on my list. I also spoke with the attorneys and advocates for the victims and the victims themselves, as well as the few abusers who would talk to me. Then I spent two full months in Rome to inquire into sexual activity among the clerics of the Vatican itself, as well as the response of Vatican authorities—including the pope—to the sex-abuse problem. It was not an uplifting pilgrimage, not for an Oregon farm boy from a devout Catholic family, not for the youth who had mystic religious experiences during devotions in the small-town church in Beaverton, Oregon.

Before I had finished that research, however, the problem exploded into a church-wide crisis, beginning in Boston and spreading across America and Europe. Soon many of the bishops were publicly exposed for abuse and cover-up, and my findings lost much of their currency for publication. My decision: to make a U-turn and head for Ireland; find out why, in the citadel of Catholicism, native son Anthony O'Connell had become one of the worst abusers in the American hierarchy; and determine, if possible, how and why so many abusers like him had been produced in that country and exported to America.

But why pick on the Irish? I had no reason to question the integrity and morality of the Irish "fathers" I had known. O'Keefe was the pastor in the church of my boyhood, where I took the water and wine to the altar as a server at his masses. Casey presided over the marriage of my wife and me. Goodrich was the head of a nearby boys' school where my grandmother worked—more on him later. Fleming was the adviser for our Christian Family Movement group of young couples seeking social justice.

Still, the stories of sexual abuse and sexual involvements in Ireland were beginning to come out in newspapers and books and on television. They seemed to mirror the problems in America. Yes, there were the love affairs of Bishop Casey and the popular priest Cleary, the egregious abuses of Smyth and Fortune, and the slave-like conditions for girls and women at the Magdalen laundries, not to mention the abuse and neglect of boys at the industrial schools. Almost all of it was perpetrated by priests, religious brothers and nuns, and all within a tiny island country with a population about the size of that in Minnesota.

I wouldn't be able to tell whether there was more abuse among Irish priests than among the Germans, French, Italians and Poles. There were no studies to make that case one way or the other. But based on all the information at hand, I suspected that the problem was far worse for the Irish.

So I went to Ireland to try to answer the key question: *Why?* Why so much abuse in this Catholic nation? And would the answer in Ireland help to explain the high level of abuse in America, especially among the Irish priests? After all, missionary priests from Ireland helped build the American Catholic Church, and Irish-American clergymen are still a dominant force in the church. Have they also been a crippling force as part of the sex-abuse scandal?

Seeking answers to these questions, in Ireland I talked to priests, journalists, and experts, as well as a leading bishop and many lay citizens. As you would expect, I combined my work with tourist stops in that lovely country, from Dingle and Galway to Limerick and Dublin. This was journalism at its most enjoyable and exciting. Back in America, I developed a database of abusive priests from Ireland, consulted with advocates for abuse victims, perused the files of the court cases, spoke with victims and their attorneys. In both countries I read all the relevant literature. And in my earlier research in Rome for my project on bishops, I had come up with information that would relate to the relationship between the Polish pope, John Paul II, and his beloved Ireland.

From all that effort and more, I came up with some answers to my questions, including a plausible, though not conclusive, answer to the big "why" of so much abuse. I also developed fully textured profiles of some of the abusers, from boy-loving Bishop O'Connell who had never dated girls in Ireland and then found sexual satisfaction with teenage boys in America, to the pedophile priest O'Grady who had been molested by two priests in his home country and later wished that his bishops in America had stopped him from abusing dozens of girls and boys. Then there was Irish-born Behan, who was stripped of his priestly duties over abuse allegations, but who still prays daily and maintains his faith. More telling, however, were the stories of the many victims, who suffered for long their encounters with the priests, some to fight back to regain their emotional stability, if not their faith in the church.

For the Irish, it has been a tragic turn of history. According to a best-selling book, *How the Irish Saved Civilization*, this people of myth and mysticism saved Europe from the barbarians during the dark ages.[2] Centuries later, thousands of Irish priests went to the United States to help preserve and spread the Catholic faith, building churches, developing an education system and serving the religious needs of the millions of immigrants who preceded them.[3]

But now I present evidence, sadly and even reluctantly, that many priests of Irish heritage helped to cripple the church they had once built, joining in what Tony Flannery calls, in both countries, a "pedophilia paradise." Through their sexual abuse and exploitation of girls, boys and women, they smashed the idealized image, portrayed so lovingly in black-and-white Hollywood movies, of the universally "good" Irish priest. I say this with great sadness, because as a Catholic I have known and read about many truly good Irish priests, who not only tended to the needs of their parishes, but worked tirelessly for social justice and the common good, knowing how their people had suffered from injustice in years past.

I should make it clear at the outset that, while Irish priests figured prominently in the American scandals, I do not contend that they were the dominant or only major factor. Rather, I offer this account of the Irish involvement because the religion and culture of this small, heavily Catholic country can be examined closely to see why so many of its priests became sexual abusers.

As we all know, Ireland's influence in literature, the arts, and world affairs has far exceeded what could be expected from a nation so small. The tragedy is that this also is true of its impact on the scandals of the Catholic priesthood, in its role as a seedbed of abuse.

PROLOGUE

THE ROMAN CATHOLIC bishop from Ireland was normally charming and gregarious; now he was somber and sweating. Flanked by two dozen loyal priests, Anthony J. O'Connell appeared at a news conference in his cathedral church in Florida to confess that he had once sexually abused two boys and was tendering his resignation to the pope. The people of his Palm Beach diocese were shocked; some cried for their bishop. They also could have cried for their church, and maybe some did, for Anthony O'Connell represented more than just one man's fall in disgrace. He also was a symbol of a church that was rapidly descending into an abyss of abuse, a free-fall that would destroy its moral authority and shake the faith of its members, in both his home country, Ireland, and in America.[1]

On March 8, 2002, O'Connell was the first American bishop to go down in the wake of a clergy-abuse explosion in Boston two months earlier, an explosion that would soon spread across America into the worst scandal in the history of the American church. In the latest count, more than 6,000 priests have been accused of sexually abusing almost 14,000 children and adolescents, at a cost to the church of $2 billion in payments to victims.[2] Many bishops took part in the abuse, condoned it, and covered it up, while showing little concern about the suffering of victims. Even before then, Catholic Ireland was reeling from reports of abuse in its boarding schools and churches. Priests, nuns and religious brothers were being convicted of abuse; an estimated 3,000 victims could claim more than $350 million in compensation, according to reports in the news media. And that was only the beginning. Many other Irish priests had gone to America to serve their church, where they played a major part in the American scandal, soiling the reputation of their church on another continent. O'Connell was one of them.

At the news conference confessing his guilt, however, O'Connell appeared to represent the best of the Irish even in the worst of times. He gave an impression of openness and honesty; he was not defensive; he apologized sincerely and abjectly. He professed to have been stupid and foolish. He asked for prayers of support. And he insisted that his intentions were good, to help the boys resolve doubts about their sexual orientation.

Still, his hometown newspaper in Ireland reported that, "The admission by the bishop has devastated family members and friends in the closely knit community of Ballynacally to which he returned on a regular basis. According to a family spokesman: shock, hurt and disbelief has been the reaction." The reaction in Palm Beach, thousands of miles away, was much the same.

If the people were shocked over his story as he told it, they had reason to be doubly shocked when his full story was revealed in the news media. Indeed, the bishop had been far less open and honest than he seemed to be. For two decades, in fact, he had been a serial sexual predator.

Anthony O'Connell straddled the ocean, with one foot in an Irish society of many abusers, and another in the American church that harbored so many of them. Accordingly, as I suggest in the introduction, he is a prism through which to view the crimes of the other priests, to seek answers to why they committed them, and to look for the links between the culture and church of their two countries. This story, then, will be told partly through the life of this skinny Irish kid who became a rotund priest lying naked with boys and young men in America.

But the prism represented by Anthony O'Connell, the most prominent of the abusers, offers only a half-light on the full spectrum of abuse in the two countries, because we don't know what in his Irish past caused him to become a sexual predator in America. We know much more about another priest, Oliver O'Grady, who was abused as a boy in his church and family, and went on to become an uncontrolled abuser, a pedophile, across the ocean.

I'll begin this narrative with an account of the infamous O'Grady, who, even more than O'Connell, helped cripple the American church. After that I'll look at the history of the migration of Irish priests and their unusual penchant to abuse girls and women, raising questions about the church's emphasis on homosexuality among American priests as the cause of the abuse crisis. Then I'll examine the life of O'Connell as an unremarkable youth in Ireland, followed by his priesthood in America, where he broke loose to develop many sexual relationships with gay young men.

In the rest of this book I will describe how Ireland became a seedbed of priestly abusers, offering for the first time evidence of how the sexual repression of cultural and clerical celibacy led to a high rate of sexual abuse in society and the priesthood. I'll also point out how Pope John Paul II overlooked the abuses in Ireland, just as he overlooked sexual misconduct in his Vatican. Finally, I will show how this story continues, for the church and for me, personally.

The new pope himself gave me a belated mandate for my work. At a meeting in Rome in 2006, Benedict XVI spoke to Irish bishops about the "deep wounds" caused by sex abuse in the Irish church and the need to rebuild confidence and trust. "In your continuing efforts to deal effectively with this problem," he said, "it is important to establish the truth of what happened in the past, to take whatever steps are necessary to prevent it from happening again, to ensure that the principles of justice are fully respected and, above all, to bring healing to the victims and to all those affected by these egregious crimes."[3]

I had already been there, "seeking the truth."

CHAPTER ONE

An Irish
Pedophile

THE AMOUNT OF THE SETTLEMENT was astounding: more than $660 million to be paid to more than 500 sexual-abuse victims in the American Catholic Church. It was announced in July of 2007, just as I was finishing this book. The settlement involved 220 priests in Los Angeles, which has an unusually large number of Irish-born clerics—and abusers. By agreeing to the payments, Cardinal Roger Mahony avoided the public trials that would have exposed his role in the sexual misconduct of his priests.

The bishops of California had recruited many of the Irish priests on promises of God and mammon, of prosperous parishes and fancy cars, of a way out of the poverty of their homeland. Many of the priests took advantage of the material benefits; but some also partook of forbidden pleasures in this garden of Eden—sex with girls and boys, women and men. Of course it was more than just sex; much of it was abusive sex, sex with children, sex of the worst kind.

One of those priests was Oliver O'Grady, who left Ireland for California in the early 1970s. Over the next 20 years, O'Grady would molest or attempt to molest up to 50 children, would eventually serve seven years in prison for his crimes, would cost his church over $13 million so far in compensation for the claims of victims, and would wind up being kicked out of the country.[1] The O'Grady case, said Tom Doyle, another Irish priest and critic, illustrates the "overall pathology of the clerical culture."[2]

I had read about O'Grady before my trip to Ireland, but there were two things I did not know—both especially significant. First, O'Grady reflected an unusual predilection characteristic of Irish abusers: an attraction to girls as well as boys. In Ireland, I learned that half the Irish priests in a large sample molested girls and young women, double the rate for American priests.[3] Second, O'Grady reflected the influence of a disturbing prevalence of sexual abuse in Irish society, some at the hands of priests, but more from family members, friends and acquaintances, and strangers. A major study in Ireland found that 30 percent of women and 24 percent of men had experienced some form of sexual abuse as children—a finding that was termed "shocking."[4] O'Grady fit the profile both as victim and perpetrator.

Amazingly, O'Grady gave the account of his own career of abuse. He told his story in two days of questioning in Ireland as part of legal proceedings on behalf of his victims. In my many years as a journalist, and then four years investigating sex abuse in the church, I have never seen such a revealing personal account by a clergy sex offender. As could be expected, O'Grady's formative years as a child are the key to understanding the man. One of six children, his father died when he was a first grader, and his mother struggled to raise her family on her own. It is possible to see how this child without a father, looking upon a priest as an authority figure known as "father," was initiated into sexual deviancy at the groping hands of two priests and his own brother. He was only 12 when the first priest began sexually touching him as he was changing clothes after serving as an altar boy at Catholic mass—the most sacred of Catholic ceremonies. At about the same time, his older brother Anthony began molesting him and his sister, who was nine. Oliver became curious about what Anthony was doing to his sister, and also began fondling her. This family abuse continued intermittently for four years. Later, as a seminary student, brother Anthony molested Oliver again while wearing clerical garments. Soon after, another priest entered the picture, becoming the second father figure to abuse Oliver, then 16, touching his genitals and arousing him sexually.

That's the way Oliver O'Grady described his bizarre and tragic early education in sex, within his family and church.

In graphic detail, O'Grady also described how the first priest had groomed him for the sexual encounter, a lesson he would apply to many children when he was a priest:

> It was after mass; he was chatting. He began the conversation by asking how I was, what I was going to do for the day. . . . [H]e called me over to him and he began to hug me you know, in a kind of gentle way first of all. Then he turned me around, which means I had my back to him and him standing behind me, and then the hands would come down and hug me there and then went lower than that.

O'Grady told how the priest first touched him sexually through his clothes, then inside his pants. The priest followed by placing Oliver's hand on the priest's genitals, until the 12-year-old stopped it. "I'm not too sure I understood what I would have been doing, believe it or not," he said.

And so, out of this abusive childhood was born a pedophile—a pedophile who, a decade after the encounter with the second priest, would be ordained a priest himself and would leave for America. He would take with him a strong compulsion for sexual contacts with children. He also would carry a subconscious feeling that "this kind of behavior was okay, or at least was not inappropriate." To him, it was the "normal thing" he had experienced as a child. Indeed, research suggests that pedophilia in fact may run in families, either as learned behavior or as a product of genetics.[5]

Among his first victims, soon after his 1971 arrival in Stockton, Calif., would be girls similar in age to the sister he had molested years earlier. He preferred sweet, innocent, playful, affectionate girls, prior to puberty, not aggressive ones who might challenge him. And he would apply what he had learned from the priest, on how to groom or seduce them for abuse. As he described it in his own words, he would make them comfortable with affectionate conversation such as, "'Hi Sally, how you doing? Come here, I

13

want to give you a hug; you are a sweetheart you know that, you are very special to me. I like you a lot.' She might respond, 'I like you,' and that would allow me to give a better hug."

And a "better hug" might prompt him to do more. "If she had a short dress, or something like that, I might have attempted to, and often did raise her dress in a subconscious way, or should I say . . . in a way that she is not aware that I'm doing that, checking her out at the same time, you get a glimpse of her underwear."

Sometimes, he said, he would get a "special lift or feeling" from seeing a girl's underwear and would continue hugging her without doing any more. (At times, O'Grady would wear women's underwear himself.)

On occasion, however, his compulsion to satisfy his sexual needs would cause him to do more. This happened one night when an 11-year-old girl, whom he had met at a summer camp, stayed over in a bedroom of his rectory. He woke up in the middle of the night and visited her in her room. "I remember going into her bed, and . . . I tried to be affectionate with her by kissing her on the mouth, and I know that my hand went down and I think I brought up her nightdress, and . . . I did touch her in the genital area outside her clothing first, and . . . I probably tried to put my hand inside her underwear." At that point, he claimed, he sensed her non-verbal objections and left her room.

As an adult, that girl—Nancy Sloan—told a newspaper reporter about other encounters with O'Grady. As she described it, he also groped between her legs at a swimming pool, forcibly kissed her in a church after performing a wedding ceremony, and fondled her at the state capitol. Her parents approved of the time she spent with O'Grady, Sloan said, because they considered it a great honor that the priest would take such personal interest in their daughter.

In the legal proceeding, O'Grady admitted that Sloan had later confronted him about his actions at the pool, told him that his hugging her and holding her down had caused her great stress, and "that she felt that she could not in any way seem to get out of that situation." He added, however, "If she said that I raped her, by which I mean penetration of the vagina, I would deny that."[6]

O'Grady was able to push aside any inhibitions when he rushed into abusive behavior, but when it was over he paid a personal price. "Shortly afterwards I would know right there and then that was wrong. I would feel often depressed, sad, angry with myself, mad at the fact that I could not control this thing or wish this thing away. That became a lot of my mental attitude and state during those years when I was trying to deal with that particular problem."

So lacking in control was O'Grady, however, that he molested a daughter and three sons of a family of nine children. He abused two children from another family, including a nine-month-old girl who doctors would find later showed vaginal scarring consistent with digital penetration. Was this man a monster? He did not appear to be. In fact, like some other Irish priests I came across in my research, he was attractive to women, developing sexual relationships with the mothers in those two families, while—unknown to them—sexually abusing their children. These were truly family affairs, in the most tragic and pathological sense. O'Grady conceded that he may have engaged in sex with mothers to gain access to their children, though he didn't think he did.[7]

A monster? Maybe. Yet, he showed the mothers and their children that he cared for them. As one of them later recounted, he came across as a caring person. "He had this quality of seeming to always be absolutely listening to you, of hearing everything, being emotionally supportive, feeding you the things you needed to hear." As is often the case with clergy abusers, however, even close associates didn't know the real Oliver O'Grady. "Everyone liked Oliver," said Cornelius DeGroot, who was the pastor of a church where O'Grady served. "But he kept people at a distance. You could never really get to know him."[8]

Tony Flannery is worth quoting at length on this point:

While the sexual abuse of a child by a priest or religious, or indeed by any

15

adult, is somewhat inexplicable, even revolting, yet . . . attempts to portray abusers as beasts and demons do not really fit the reality as I have known it. I have known, and even for periods of time lived with, some of the priests who have been convicted of abuse, and in many ways they were good, kind and caring individuals. That is the complex reality of child abuse that we as society have yet to come to grips with. If it were beasts and demons who did these things it would be much easier to deal with. Instead they seem to be people who are perfectly ordinary, and even good, in other aspects of their lives."[9]

I can vouch for Flannery's observation from personal knowledge. I remember a priest, the late Fr. John Goodrich, director of St. Mary's Home for Boys near our family farm in the environs of Beaverton, Oregon. He was widely admired and respected as a brilliant preacher and charismatic caretaker of Catholic boys, a priest who went to Ireland every year, who said he loved only two women, his mother and the sexually pure Virgin Mary. As an altar boy and fervent Catholic at the time, I was inspired by the sermons and the image of this handsome, dynamic man. My Grandma Rigert also knew him because she worked for him, mending clothes for the boys in a small corner room. She was saving money to support the education of a future priest after a son rejected a priestly career. Goodrich should have been a model for her vision of the priest who would fulfill her lifelong dream.

But he was not that model. Years later it was revealed in a lawsuit that he had been abusing boys, and developing a long-time sexual relationship with at least one, at a cost to the church of a settlement for almost $2 million.[10] My grandmother did not live to see him come crashing down, but maybe she would not have been surprised. She didn't like him, possibly because boys had told her what he was doing. And he had asked her to leave, possibly because he feared she knew too much. After he was exposed for the man he was, the tell-tale signs were recalled, that boys had been seen going through the garage to his room, that pictures of shirtless boys were seen on the walls in the room no one else was allowed to enter. At the end, he was observed in a nursing home, a shriveled old man, a shadow of the priest he had been—or had pretended to be. By then I had no more illusions about the sanctity of some of these revered figures of my childhood.

Like Goodrich, O'Grady was not seen as a monster, but his account shows that he was, at the least, a very sick and twisted man. He excused himself for molesting some of the children in the belief they were flirting with him, even seducing him into doing sexual acts. Little children flirting? Well, he said, it was like the boy dropping his towel and exposing his genitals after drying off at the swimming pool. Some pedophiles are so deluded they think the children enjoy the sexual acts.[11] One of O'Grady's counselors said he was sexually immature—a rather obvious observation. But was he so immature that he thought the children were partly to blame for their abuse at his own hands? Or was he like the politicians who come to feel a lie is the truth, if they repeat it often enough? There is no way to know.

The most important question is how O'Grady got away with molesting children for two decades without being revealed as the pedophile he was. I'll list three reasons. First, this relatively short man with thinning hair appeared to be so non-threatening. Second, his victims were too shamed and felt too guilty to tell anyone. And third, this being the most important reason of all, church authorities—three bishops in O'Grady's case—covered up the abuse to avoid scandal, escape legal jeopardy and protect their own reputations, regardless of the harm to children, harm that damaged some of them for life.

O'Grady admitted that as early as the mid-1970s he molested Nancy Sloan, but he suffered no repercussions. On the contrary, his bishop, Merlin Guilfoyle, was upset that O'Grady had apologized in writing to her parents, placing the church in legal jeopardy. In 1984, O'Grady again admitted that he had molested a child, this time a boy, but Guilfoyle's successor, Bishop Roger Mahony, was similarly dismissive of the continuing O'Grady problem, even promoting him to be pastor in charge of his parish. Later, when he was finally called to account in a civil lawsuit accusing his diocese of harboring a pedophile, Mahony admitted no culpability, claimed he knew nothing, and defended his actions. No, he never saw O'Grady's 1976 letter admitting the abuse of a girl, which was in his church files. No, he didn't know the details of what O'Grady told a therapist in 1984 about abusing a boy. No, in fact, he didn't even speak to the therapist about O'Grady's "confession." No, no, no. In a church in which accountability is a foreign concept, Mahony was not about to take any responsibility for the crimes of his priest, or consider the harm to children. Two jurors in the trial later concluded that he was lying.[12]

If Mahony was not loyal to the truth, he had certainly been loyal to his priest. After O'Grady had three times admitted his criminal behavior, and after Mahony had transferred him to another parish, the bishop wrote a letter to "Dear Oliver." "Thank you very much," he wrote, "for your very beautiful letter of January 3, and I was so pleased to read the spirit and enthusiasm which you have in your life at this time, for the direction in which the Lord is calling you. You have been such a part of my prayer constantly and, I assure you of those continuing prayers for the future." The bishop went on express a desire to be of more help to his priest. He signed it off with, "Assuring you of my prayers and with kindest personal regards, yours fraternally in Christ."[13]

In a new parish, where Mahony promoted him to be pastor, O'Grady went on to abuse more children, while the bishop also was promoted, to head the huge Los Angeles archdiocese and later to don the red robes of cardinal, a prince of his church.

Not all clerics, I should note, were so blind to the problem of abusive priests. As early as the 1950s, an Irish priest warned about the need for bishops to deal forcefully with the abusers. Fr. Gerald Fitzgerald, who had founded a treatment center in New Mexico for alcoholic priests, proposed to banish the "devils" who seduced boys and girls to a Caribbean island. If he were a bishop, he wrote at the time, he would tremble if he failed to report an abuser to Rome to be defrocked. "It is for this class of rattlesnake I have always wished the island retreat," Fitzgerald continued, "but even an island is too good for these vipers of whom the Gentle Master said—it is better they had not been born."[14] An archbishop rejected his plan.

Even if his proposal was a bit extreme, Fitzgerald recognized the severity of the problem. On the contrary, bishops like Mahony simply covered up the problem and failed to take any personal responsibility. It's an oft-told story in this tragic saga of a corrupted church.

If we can believe what he said in retrospect, O'Grady would have preferred that the bishops had taken responsibility in his case. He expressed the wish that church authorities had helped him stop the abuse by taking him out of the ministry, rather than moving him from one parish to another. He pointed out that they didn't offer or pay for any specialized residential treatment, leaving him alone as long as no criminal or civil action was taken against him. What they were doing, he said, was looking out for themselves. Then, when he was arrested and sent to prison, he felt they had abandoned him. "I felt I was on my own," he said.

Some of his reaction seems self-serving, as though O'Grady could not at the time demand that church authorities do more to help him help himself. And the bishops had taken some steps to deal with his problem: they sent him to three different therapists; told him to stay away from one child and her family; transferred him to a parish that had no school (though it had hundreds of children attending religion classes). But all these efforts were perfunctory, like telling a troublesome school child to go to the principal's office and be good. None of it amounted to a serious attempt to stop the abuse. In some ways, the bishops were enabling him.

O'Grady's claim that he tried to help himself also seems a bit self-serving. True, he sought counseling on his initiative, read books to understand his disorder, attended meetings for sex addicts. But it's hard to sympathize with this priest after he says, in a preposterous statement of naiveté, that he would like to have been "advised that this particular lifestyle would not be the best way to go." Are we to believe he had to be told that it was monumentally wrong to damage or destroy the lives of children, many of them little ones? After all, he also said his religion had taught him that this behavior was wrong and sinful. And as a believing Catholic, he probably confessed his sins to another priest, freeing him of guilt and leaving him free to go out and sin again. After all, the confidentiality of confession would prevent his fellow priest from telling anyone that he was a pedophile. Breaking the sacred seal of confession is considered one of the worst sins in the church.

Looking back after he left prison, O'Grady said he never should have been a priest. Of course, that admission came far too late after twenty years of abuse, leaving one victim suicidal and countless others with profound emotional problems. Should we feel sorry for this priest, a product of a sexually dysfunctional childhood? It's a common conundrum: should the serial killer, or the serial sex abuser, be partly excused because of his horrible background? I don't think it excuses the crime, but it should be considered in judging the criminal. Either way, in the O'Grady case there was no justification for allowing this pedophile priest to continue destroying the lives of children, whatever caused him to do it. He should have been stopped, and he could have been. He said so himself.

O'Grady's career as a pedophile was brought to a halt, finally, because two boys, by then adults, went to police and forced the church to act—and compelled him to plead guilty. One of their parents was a mother who had been seduced by O'Grady in counseling over marital difficulties. It is fitting that the criminal case that prompted him to plead guilty involved boys, because he had molested far more boys than girls, though the abuse of girls is what set him—and many of his countrymen—apart from most other American clergy abusers. Oliver O'Grady was not the homosexual targeted by Vatican authorities as the cause of the sex-abuse problem. He identified himself as heterosexual, which seems accurate considering he abused children of both sexes. Trying to keep homosexuals from joining the priesthood, as the Vatican is trying to do, would not put a stop to the Oliver O'Gradys of the ministry.[15]

But O'Grady finally was forced out of the priesthood. When he got out of prison, after serving half of his 14-year-sentence, he was immediately put on a plane to the country where he had started on his tragic course. When attorneys for victims found him, he was living in Ireland on disability payments after a heart attack, bypass surgery and pancreatitis. By then, after a lot of therapy, he was ashamed and embarrassed over the "terrible wrong" he had done. But when John Manly, attorney for many of the victims, asked if he would apologize to the victims, pleading with him to do so in the name of the "Blessed Mother," he could not say the three words, "I am sorry." As the priest put it, he might apologize later but doing so during litigation would put him in jeopardy for admitting guilt. "Therefore the victim, if they have a lawsuit, can gain money out of this, do you understand?" How much money? "Millions of dollars," he said.

One could ask, however, why O'Grady was so concerned about whether the victims would make money out of his admissions of guilt. The money would not come from him; he had no "millions." The money would come from the church and/or its insurers. A more likely explanation for his reluctance to admit to any more guilt is that the church had bought him off. Whereas O'Grady had first opposed an effort by the diocese to take away his priestly powers, figuring the church was seeking to duck its own responsibility for the harm he had done, he agreed to be defrocked later. He changed his mind after the church offered him an annuity of $800 a month when he turned 65 (in 2010).

By that time, O'Grady was also backing off from some of the claims of abuse, admitting only that he had touched or fondled the victims. Manly, who had been deferential in much of the earlier questioning, stated: "[A] number of the victims, including my client, said that you anally penetrated them, and they anally penetrated you. And that you ejaculated in front of them. Do you take issue with that?" The priest said that he did. Manly pressed him, "Why do you think almost all of the victims describe their abuse as worse than you are characterizing it?" The priest's answer: "Simply put, the worse the scenario the more the money they are going to get." In this late stage of the questioning, Manly called him a liar, and O'Grady didn't deny it.

O'Grady also acknowledged at that time that he was a pedophile—an easy admission considering his record. More recently, an American film documentary, "Deliver Us From Evil," brought more public attention to his admitted guilt and prompted more alleged victims to bring civil lawsuits. After the film was released in 2006, while he was living in Ireland, he moved four times in two years and cut off contact with the news media, becoming a man on the run.[16]

CHAPTER TWO

PRIESTS AND CHILDREN

THE LONG, COLD WINTERS and lack of priests made it difficult for some of these Irish "fathers" to perform their Catholic duties in the missionary territories of northern America. In upper New York state, often less than half the scattered parishioners could attend mass because of bad weather, with temperatures remaining below zero for weeks on end.[1] It was no better in the desolate areas of western Washington state, which was quite a contrast to the Ireland from whence these priests had come—a land partly warmed by the Gulf Stream and blessed with a surplus of priests to serve the millions of faithful. But the Irish migrants came with a mission to sustain them: to save souls.

While studying for the priesthood in Ireland, James O'Malley wrote to Bishop Charles White of Spokane, Washington, on July 1, 1943, "I hope with God's grace to prepare myself during the coming years, that I may be a priest possessed with apostolic zeal and ready to work hard for souls to save them for God."[2]

Three decades later, Fr. Liam O'Doherty, a priest in the diocese of Ogdensburg, New York, would write to his seminary in Ireland, "The North Country has its drawbacks, but the saving of souls is what counts here. And saving souls is a little more difficult in this modern American society."[3]

What they didn't mention was the challenge of saving their own souls. O'Malley was accused much later of sexually abusing at least 15 boys from the late 1950s until he retired in 1989 and returned to Ireland. "He was allowed to molest kids for more than 30 years," said Rick Frizzell, an alleged victim and retired state trooper. "He had his hands down their pants all the time." One lawsuit against the church has been settled; others are pending.[4]

O'Doherty was accused of molesting more than 20 girls and two women over a period of more than two decades, rivaling the crimes of the infamous Oliver O'Grady in California. O'Doherty denied it all, but the diocese of Ogdensburg eventually paid $180,000 to settle lawsuits brought by four of the victims, stripped him of his priestly privileges, and sent him to a facility for troubled priests.[5]

Way back in the 1940s, Bishop White knew he had a problem with the Irish priests, but he didn't know how bad it would get. He had written then that "more than one-half of the men that I have gotten from Irish seminaries have gone on the rocks, two of whom have given up their priesthood and attempted marriage."[6] On the other hand, he said, "We have other Irish priests who are among our most outstanding pastors of souls."[7] Sixty years after White wrote, the diocese of Spokane agreed to pay $48 million to victims of clergy sex abuse; O'Malley was one of the abusers.[8]

O'Malley, O'Doherty and O'Grady are among the many priests who led me to conclude that Irish-born clergy helped cripple the American Catholic Church through their participation in its massive sex abuse scandal. I base that partly on my estimate that close to 5 percent of them molested minors.[9] It is true that my estimates show the total number of Irish abusers to be relatively small, probably in the low hundreds. But the actual total, while unknown, could be much higher. I say this because the public accusations of abuse, which are the basis of my estimates of Irish misconduct, do not include the many cases never reported by victims, or by church officials.

Many additional cases have been revealed later in civil lawsuits. Catholic officials in Los Angeles, for example, reported that Irish-born priests accounted for a whopping 14 percent of sex-abuse lawsuits (18 of 126) in that archdiocese, which has the nation's largest Catholic population.[10] The new pope, Benedict XVI, was said to have been pained and concerned by the "devastating scale" of the problem in Los Angeles, a pain that must have been exacerbated by the $660 million settlement for victims that was forced on the church.

The involvement of the Irish is much, much greater when priests of Irish ancestry, as well as those from Ireland, are counted. Then they make up one-third of the 2,000 priests publicly accused of sex abuse in America, giving them a huge role in this darkest of tragedies in their church.[11]

I could go on with numbers and speculation as to what they mean, but for now I will focus on the stories behind the numbers, stories of priestly depravity illustrated in case after case of the abuses of these men from Ireland. While many preached a strict sexual morality, they practiced a gross immorality.

Rosemary Beck, now 76 years old, of Ontario, California, told me that a priest made the sign of the cross and blessed her even as he was groping her. She had "blacked out" the memory of this abuse for more than 60 years—it happened in 1939, when she was a sixth grader—but finally she wanted somebody to know. Even now, she said, it haunts her "as bad as before."

Rosemary's story carries a special significance. As I noted in the first chapter, half of these priests have been accused of molesting girls, double the rate for American priests of all backgrounds.[12] I found that an even higher percentage of the sex-abuse lawsuits in Los Angeles involved girls.[13] I submit that the alleged victims in these lawsuits, girls and boys, paid a high price for the fact that the Los Angeles church recruited so many priests from Ireland. For example, more students from the Carlow seminary were sent to Los Angeles than any other U.S. diocese.[14] Los Angeles church officials also did a hard sell at the Jesuit Mungret College in Limerick. Kevin Laheen, a former student, told me that the archbishop of Los Angeles, James Francis McIntyre, later to be a cardinal, would come to Mungret promising that the young men would soon be driving Cadillacs if they signed up.[15] "A lot of the inducement was materialistic—cars and money," added Donal Gannon, former teacher. "A student would say 'my mother at home is very poor,' and the bishop would fork over some money."[16]

Some of these young men became "good" priests, but others, as Bishop White warned, went on the rocks. One of them was Father George Foley, a member of the Sacred Heart congregation, who got in trouble, as the Los Angeles archdiocese put it, over "women and wine," the very problem that White had complained about. When the Los Angeles diocese released a list of its errant priests, it gave these details: "An adult female writes . . . alleging that she was sexually abused by Fr. Foley as a minor (from approximately 1971–74), while Fr. Foley was staying with her and having sexual relations with her mother."

In her lawsuit against the church, Foley's victim, Mia Lynn Giorgi, made some remarkable claims: that the priest inflicted almost every kind of sexual act on her, that his superiors were aware that he was living at Giorgi's home, and that many of his colleagues in the priesthood knew he was living at her home and visited him there. Suddenly, the lawsuit said, Foley's Sacred Heart congregation transferred him to England.[17]

Another priest from Ireland who came much later to Bishop White's territory in eastern Washington also showed that the bishop's warning was prescient. Father Michael Simpson was an alcoholic who allegedly abused at least eight girls—probably more. Two women said he abused them more than 40 years earlier; one claiming he raped her at age ten.[18] News of a lawsuit prompted a third woman to tell the church: "He liked little girls, which I know first hand. He made me recite the ten commandments in front of my catechism class while he had his hands in my underwear . . . I was about nine years old. I told, as did many other young girls, but of course no one believed he meant any harm. I handled it myself by not going anywhere near him."[19] Attorney Tim Kosnoff of Seattle, Washington, told me, "We have five [more] women that have accused him and we are still digging. . . . He apparently preferred nine-year-old girls. It was a consistent pattern; he'd trap them in the rectory and digitally rape them."[20] Simpson eventually returned to Ireland, suffering from a raging alcoholism that probably would have taken his life if cancer hadn't done so first.

Kosnoff, who obtained the documents on Bishop White's concerns, asked me this question about the Irish priests: "Why were so many of them child molesters, drunks and misfits? Was this a conscious decision by the seminaries to export the trash, or was what was sent to the U.S. representative of the kinds of men Irish seminaries were producing?"[21]

It's harsh language, but not entirely unjustified, at least as related to some, even if a small minority, of the exports. As early as the 1800s, writes historian Lawrence McCaffrey, bishops in Ireland had exiled many priests for misconduct involving drink or women or disobedience. "Frequently they continued to indulge their vices or disruptive attitudes and behavior in the United States," causing scandal and discontent.[22] Another historian notes that Irish priests at that time were also accusing each other and their bishops of scandalous behavior, including sexual irregularities.[23]

In the following years, and well into the 1900s, the Irish seminaries were churning out thousands of clergymen for the churches in America. But these priests weren't necessarily of the highest quality. In a two-class system, the top candidates for the priesthood were channeled to the national seminary in Maynooth for service in Ireland. As a disgruntled priest put it, "Those of us who were average were left out and were advised to look elsewhere," which for many meant going to seminaries producing priests for the United States and other countries.[24] Were these "second-class" priests more prone to be abusive? I can't say. But as I noted above, Bishop White in Spokane expressed great concern about the problem in the 1940s.

More recently, Irish Catholic authorities sent pedophile Brendan Smyth to North Dakota without telling the bishop there of his problems.[25] Oliver O'Grady had been found unfit for the priesthood by an Irish religious order, but was ordained anyway and shipped to the states, where he continued his predatory practices.[26] Just as egregious is the case of Bishop Anthony O'Connell, who had been turned down by 36 American bishops, by his own count, until he was accepted by a newly formed diocese in Missouri, where a friend told him "the bishop was so desperate he would take anyone." (Surprisingly, and to his credit, that is what O'Connell himself told a newspaper reporter.) O'Connell didn't say why he was repeatedly rejected, but he went on to be accused as priest and bishop of abusing at least nine boys and young men, before resigning in disgrace.[27]

It would be wrong, of course, to treat these priests out of context, without recognizing the great contributions of so many of their colleagues. The Missionary College of All Hallows in Ireland, commemorating its 150th anniversary, wrote about its priests abroad, "They worked against considerable odds—poverty, isolation, loneliness, disease, racial prejudice, religious bigotry—but their labors were none the less effective. The present powerful and imposing edifice of the Catholic Church in America is a monument to the toilsome labor and patient endeavor of these self-sacrificing men." One bishop from All Hallows counted 11,000 "souls" he had confirmed in the faith in Texas.[28]

By the same token, however, it would be wrong to discount the horrible harm that a sizeable number of these priests, honored as "fathers," representatives of Jesus Christ, men of God, inflicted on children across America—boys and girls in equal numbers. The abuse of children of either sex is terribly harmful. But, as I pointed out earlier, I have emphasized the targeting of girls and women by the Irish priests because it is contrary to the homosexual behavior that has been the dominant factor in the sexual abuse by American priests. Almost two-thirds of those priests molested boys only, and eight out of ten of their victims were boys. By comparison, I have estimated that one-half of the abusive priests from Ireland targeted girls, demonstrating heterosexual behavior.[29]

As for me, born into a strict Catholic family, I knew nothing of these issues in my earlier years. I didn't even think about priests having any sexual inclinations, one way or the other. Certainly, I had no idea that thousands of them, of whatever nationality or sexual orientation, were fondling, masturbating, and sexually penetrating boys, girls, and adults throughout the years that I was growing up. Almost all of this had been covered up and kept secret by the church.

All the while, my family followed the rules of the church on sexual morality without question. No birth control; my mother had thirteen children. No lustful thoughts; we had to own up to them to the priest in confession. No overt displays of sexual desire; Fr. O'Keefe sat in the back row of the local cinema to make sure the children weren't necking. Later, Fr. Michael Fleming of Ireland was in tune with an increasingly liberal culture when he served as advisor to our group of Christian families seeking social and racial justice, without reference to sexual behavior. But he was too liberal to stay under the conservative pastor Anthony Gerace. Fleming was transferred from our suburban Portland parish, exiled to a boondocks church. He later left the priesthood to marry—another "risk" cited by Bishop White so long ago.

While priestly abuses continued in secret, we Catholics retained an idealized view of our priests, like Fr. Edward Flanagan of Boy's Town (he was Irish, of course), and the other good priests portrayed by Bing Crosby and Barry Fitzgerald (both Irish) in the movies. The church, in fact, touted Crosby as the ideal Catholic father, with a lovely wife and attractive family of four boys. And, as young parents, we joined the church in efforts to root out immorality in the movies and adult bookstores. Then, in the mid-1980s, newspaper reporters, attorneys, and advocates for victims and their organizations began to break through the secrecy and expose the reality. Not even Crosby was immune: his wife was an alcoholic; three of his sons were known as Hollywood's "bad boys" because of their drinking; two of those sons later committed suicide, and another son wrote a nasty book accusing his father of child abuse and infidelity.[30] (Fr. Flanagan's sterling reputation, however, has remained intact.)

As I learned about the horrors of the sex-abuse scandal, and studied it as a journalist, I could not but conclude that the church of my past had been a deeply corrupted and even criminal institution—corrupted from the abuse that had occurred, and criminal for covering it up and allowing it to continue, even flourish.

Although many priests from Ireland and of Irish ancestry were among the more than 6,000 American clergy offenders in the last half of the twentieth century, they have so far avoided any ethnic stigma in the United States, even as clergy sex abuse blew up into a crisis within strongly Catholic Ireland itself.

Actually, the significant role of the Irish priests in the American scandal should come as no surprise, simply because priests from Ireland and of Irish ancestry have played such a dominant role in the American church. The best estimates are that 4,000 of them came to the United States, many of them recruited by Irish bishops, to serve the burgeoning Irish immigrant population and save their souls.[31] By the 1960s, at the peak of their numbers, half of the American priests and three-quarters of the bishops had come from Ireland. During this time when the American Catholic Church was predominantly Irish, in the 1960s and '70s, clergy sex abuse was also at its peak. By the year 2000, the number had declined to 1,221 priests from Ireland, but more than four out of ten American priests said they were of Irish ancestry, maintaining the strong Irish presence in the American Catholic clergy and taking part in the sexual abuse. Much of this abuse had occurred long ago but now was coming to light.[32]

A few years ago, my sister Jane asked me about the credibility of those late accusations of abuse after reading that a woman had claimed she was abused more than 40 years earlier by William Skylstad of Spokane, Washington, now a bishop and former head of the national organization of Catholic bishops.[33] (He has denied it.) Jane did not question the accusation as an apologist for the church, because she has mostly given up on the male-dominated institution and developed a personal faith. She just wanted to know why a supposed victim would wait so long to make her claim.

The question can best be answered, I suggest, by the victims themselves, in this case the young girls and often vulnerable women molested at an unusual rate by priests from Ireland. Susan Renehan was one of them. At the age of 11, she had an "innocent crush" on Father Michael Garry, an Irish priest assigned to her parish in the Trenton, N.J., diocese. One of seven children in an alcoholic home, Susan was an insecure "Irish street kid," as she put it. Garry was kind; he talked and listened to her. She was vulnerable, and Garry took advantage of that. When the priest first sexually abused her, her reaction was "shock, terror, and utter helplessness." He continued the abuse for three years, assaulting her in his car, cornering her in the school hallway and in the rectory. After he was transferred to another parish he continued to stalk her, tracking her one day after school to a coffee shop where she was waiting with girlfriends to get the train home. "When he offered to give my friends and me a ride home, I was desperate to protect them. That gave me the courage to tell him no," Susan recalls. "At the time, I was terrified. Today, I'm proud of that. That was the last time I saw him." Later she learned that he had returned to Ireland, as did many other priest abusers from America. Nonetheless, Renehan kept her sexual abuse by the priest a secret 26 years, long after he died.

This account may sound implausible; a girl going through the trauma of abuse for three years without putting a stop to it and then keeping it a secret for so long. Renehan explained it this way: "The child has no language or resources for dealing with these heinous crimes. And I had been taught that a priest was an authority figure, God's representative on earth." When Garry abused her, she would plead, "Please don't do this," but she didn't know how to make him stop. When it was over, she felt trapped by feelings of betrayal and shame, feelings that prompted her to bury it all inside. Finally, at a meeting of abuse survivors in Boston, she realized that she was a victim like many others. So for the first time she told the press about her own abuse. She had shed the shame. But she never told her parents about it, never. "I felt the need to protect them," she said. "I felt it was something they couldn't handle." They died without knowing.[34]

Many sexual predators, Irish or not, have found their prey among the youngsters who served as "altar boys," wearing the black and white garments, proudly bringing wine to the altar to be transformed by the priest, according to his church, into the blood of Christ. No priest, and certainly not the stern Fr. George O'Keefe, ever tried to approach me sexually during my time in that role; if one had, I would have been exceedingly confused, knowing so little about sex. But these boys were right there in the inner sanctum of the sacristy next to the altar, easy game for the predator priests.

If the Irish priests who sought sex preferred girls and young women, as many of them did, they had to look elsewhere. And they found them without difficulty: in confession, in Catholic schools, at summer camp, in choir practice, or in their homes during visits. They found them and molested them in every way possible, blatantly violating their trust in priests. Liam O'Doherty's victims, aged 8 to 14, said he abused them at his residence and in their home, washing and fondling them while they were bathing; forcing one to sit naked on his lap, another to sleep with him with her pants off. O'Doherty's response: "With youngsters these days, you never know what they're thinking. They visualize things through the influence of the mass media that you and I never thought of."[35]

Listen to other victims, like Laura Halford. She recalled that when she was 13 an Irish priest in confession asked if she had ever had sex. When she told him that a male cousin had raped her the previous year, "The priest... told me that I deserved to be molested because I was a bad girl. He asked me all sorts of inappropriate questions, like had I ever touched myself, did I know that I tempted men . . . stuff like that. He told me that my purpose was to be a sexual device for [him], that I had no value other than that." After hearing her confession, they sat in a private area where he molested her, she said. "The incident was so horrific you cannot imagine." Like Renehan, she kept the abuse secret for many years. "I never told anyone about it at the time—I was ashamed to my soul. I didn't come forward until I was watching an archdiocese of Baltimore training video on sexual abuse—then I just lost it and came out with it," and broke down sobbing. Yes, she went public after 25 years.

And listen to victim Nicki Rister, talking about Fr. Patrick O'Keeffe, the "great seducer" as she called him. "Pat knew I did not have any close friends and that I had just come from a girls' school. My parents suggested I go and join the church choir to help me make friends. I did and Pat—she never called him "father"—was there watching. He asked me if I would do some typing for him in the school office after school in the evenings. I said,

'Sure.' One night he gave me a 'brotherly hug' and then he kissed me. Boy was I surprised. He then had me meeting him in his office doing things I had never done before, having wine with him and eventually intercourse." She was a minor, age 17, during most of the alleged sexual activity, which included repeated acts of oral sex and, later, intercourse. She had some doubts about oral sex, she recalled, but he convinced her it was all right. As the sex went on, she said, "I would spend hours in my room crying from guilt and shame and my parents would send me over to talk to Pat." It took Rister 30 years to go public, after both parents had died.

But there is more to the Rister case than the tragedy of her "affair" with a priest (and sex with a minor is a crime, however much it may appear to be consensual). Sadly, her case shows how hard it is for a woman to get redress in complaining about a priest. Her family, her church and his native Ireland simply did not take her complaint seriously. Two sisters and her father, before he died, turned against her. Her bishop, Phillip Straling of San Bernardino, California, merely told his priest to write a letter of apology and go to another parish. O'Keeffe initiated sexual affairs with two women after that. And after he fled to Ireland in the face of felony charges, his country refused to comply with an extradition order to send him back. O'Keeffe committed no crime under Irish law, authorities said, because a 17-year-old is considered to be an adult in that country. Forget that he was accused of a crime in the United States; O'Keeffe was home free. And Rister was left behind. "I should hate you for what you have done to me," she told him in a letter. "Using me for your own physical needs and then going on your way, leaving me to cope with the guilt."

O'Keeffe did express remorse in letters to Rister, patronizingly calling her a "poor darling" and telling her to put the past in "God's hands," as if that would make everything okay. He admitted that she was a victim, but he also portrayed himself as somewhat of a victim. "I don't talk to anyone, only to God," he wrote. "Friends do not exist for me . . . I do hope that my death will come soon; it is not possible for me to be happy." Accordingly, he felt compelled to resign and was no longer a practicing priest.

Later, though, O'Keeffe denied everything in a deposition taken for a civil lawsuit brought by Rister. He denied hugging her sexually; denied kissing her; denied having oral sex or sexual intercourse with her. Rister, who was there in Dublin for part of the questioning, told me by e-mail, "Pat used to have beautiful blue eyes, but I noticed while staring at him that they are dark and empty now. Satan has taken everything from him. His soul is gone. I really don't know how he lives with himself. And he is still collecting a pension from the church!"

The ultimate irony for Rister was that her father had become a priest himself after her mother's death, and, upon hearing of her "affair" with O'Keeffe, she said that he told her, "He is a man, too, and has feelings." The men of the church take care of each other, perhaps because, but for the grace of their God, they could be the next to be accused.

O'Keeffe does not come across as a sympathetic figure, for all his expressions of sympathy for his victim. After all, according to Rister's statement to police, he had convinced her to perform oral sex on him up to 15 times, for his gratification only. And despite his self-proclaimed death wish, he was stable enough to return to Ireland to be with family. Rister ridiculed him, saying "He ran screaming like a little girl back to Ireland to hide and collect retirement pay from the church." Rister said she has moved on with her own life; she has been "very happily married to the same guy for 23 years."

In the course of my research, I found that it was not unusual for accused Irish priests to go back under the skirts of their mother country, to escape from disgrace and, in some cases, to avoid prison. In Florida some years ago, Father Edward McLoughlin left the country within 24 hours after being confronted with abuse allegations.[36] One-quarter of the abusers in my sample returned to Ireland, and at least one—the late Thomas McNamara of Jacksonville in Florida—continued molesting teenagers in Ireland.[37]

In his biting book *The Lie of the Land*, Fintan O'Toole described the migratory path of another abusive priest, Brendan Smyth. "He had been abusing children in Britain, Ireland and America since the 1950s. Each time he was sent to a parish, whispers of scandal would begin to emerge. Each time, he would be sent back to Ireland, and then posted off to another parish." O'Toole observes that when Smyth died in a gay sauna, two priests "fortunately" were present, as patrons of the sauna, to administer the last rites.[38]

The victims of priestly abuse avoided their own shame by holding it inside, until they could hold it no longer—not just to join in the many lawsuits, but to help alert others to the risks of getting close to the "men of God." As one woman said, "I don't want any compensation, apologies, etcetera from the church. I just hope these things stop happening. I'm sure it must be very widespread if I have experienced it in my limited encounters with the church. I am no longer a practicing Catholic."[39]

The fact is that many of these women emerged from their experiences as far stronger than the priests. Rister, for one, showed her fortitude by first complaining to her bishop, then to police, and then going back to the church when it showed a latter-day willingness to help her heal. Renehan went on to help create advocacy organizations for abuse survivors. They were indeed strong women; had they been allowed in the church leadership, they might have stopped much of the abuse, much earlier.

CHAPTER THREE

CONSENTING
ADULTS?

FRANK FLYNN LOVED WOMEN. Maybe it was his Irish charm and wonderful brogue that made him think he was irresistible. Or maybe it was because he thought they owed him for the way he comforted them in the midst of their personal problems. For whatever reasons, he allegedly engaged in sexual intercourse with at least three women, and grabbed, hugged and kissed others.[1]

Michael Kenny was also popular and promiscuous—he admitted being sexually involved with ten women. He took them out for movies, dancing and underage drinking; had sexual intercourse with six of them, even fathered two children.[2]

Paul Cleary was accused of breaking up a marriage and taking women into his bedroom. He also was accused of seducing a 17-year-old girl but waiting for sex until she was 18, when he could no longer be charged with abusing a minor.[3]

In the free-wheeling culture of America today, or less obviously in years past, there is nothing remarkable about sexual relationships among consenting adults. I heard many stories about these sexual encounters during my four years in the U.S. Navy, though I was not a participant. In that all-male military milieu, developing sexual involvements was rather an obsession among many of these men. They talked on and on about their "conquests."

Flynn, Kenny and Cleary were also part of an all-male institution, but with a big difference. They were priests, Irish born. As such, they were married to Jesus Christ and their church—under a vow of celibacy, committed to be chaste and to remain unmarried. So when they became involved with women, they were cheating on their partner Christ, just as some of the women, attracted to these forbidden males, were cheating on their husbands.

I don't want to get preachy about these relationships. They can be quite benign and healthy. My wife and I came to know a priest, of Irish ancestry, who would come to Minneapolis on weekends with his religious sister friend. As far as we knew, the two of them—like some other priests and nuns—simply didn't believe in celibacy. Our friend seemed to be having an honest, happy relationship. Some men have maintained these involvements while remaining in the priesthood; many others have left to get married, often with the hope that the straightjacket of celibacy eventually will be removed and they can resume priestly service.

But sexual relationships with priests are not always so benign, coequal, or consensual, not when the priest has the power and authority derived from representing the Catholic concept of God and the reputed divinity of his son Jesus Christ. And certainly, the relationship is not benign when a woman is vulnerable in counseling and the priest seduces her into an affair, then casts her off for another woman.

Garry Wills, in his book *Papal Sin*, contends that many heterosexual priests are "living a lie, gaining emotional access to women under the pretence of virtue, using and abandoning them because they cannot make a true and open commitment to a women, or conscripting them into a life of deception if they prolong a furtive affair. They . . . must observe a discipline of deceit lest their secret slip out. They are in their own prison of falsehoods."

I could have easily concluded that Frank Flynn's relationship with Pat Hittel in Florida was nothing more than the affection between consenting adults—until I talked extensively to her husband Bob, heard his side of the story, and read Pat's own account of her relationship with Flynn as described in almost a decade of diary entries. While the pedophile priest Oliver O'Grady had given a chilling account of his abuse of children under the questioning of an attorney, this adult woman Pat Hittel told, day by day, her anguished tale of an illicit love affair with her priest, a tale that ended when she died of cancer.[4]

The story of Pat, Bob and Frank, as related by the Hittels and denied by Flynn, is the story of a wife deeply in love with another man yet torn by guilt over her deception of the husband she still loved; the story of a husband who would take her to her private meetings with priest Frank, knowing nothing of their alleged affair until after she died; the story of priest Frank who led Pat into a relationship of some years, then suddenly dropped her for another woman, causing her to go into an emotional tailspin of despair. Of course, it could be just the typical story of a man or woman leaving a spouse for another mate, except for the fact that the other man was a priest, who was supposed to be a healer, not a destroyer.

Was Pat, of Irish ancestry, truly a victim of the man she professed to love passionately, the "beautiful priest" from Ireland? Pat felt that she was. After Frank left her for another woman, she expressed those feelings in repeated diary conversations with her Lord and God, writing one day of an expected phone call, "No call, Lord—he said he would. No call—what does it mean? . . . I want to trust and believe that I still count, but I guess I don't, or he thinks it is best for me." Another day, Pat wrote that she feared being cast aside and no longer loved. Seeing herself as a castoff, she then recalled that Frank had shown only passion, not love. Finally, over a period of four days in early 1985, in a conversation with "Jesus, Lord and God," she poured out her emotions about the priest and the woman who took her place:

April 14. Dear love, I have had hurt feelings about you for over two years, since Jack [Pat and Bob's son] died and you didn't come to me…I have needed more from you and she got it all—all the attention and time, the visits, the steak and wine dinners, the trips, all without me.

39

April 17. Lord, I do feel used and abused. He said it—and I feel it now. His love for her is sublime—he has made it so! His human passion for me was lust—he knew me not. Oh Lord—what do I do?

April 18. I miss him so much—how lonely I am. I can't seem to get beyond it. . . . I felt old, used, abused, two, three or four women. Not me the beloved. I felt him a scoundrel. I felt he just wanted her and all of us could go to hell. . . . She seems to be more important to him than me. . . . I have wanted what she had, a place in his life, in his parish. I feel I have been pushed out and not wanted. . . . I realize that I was wanting and needing him to be all that my father and husband never were to me; neither of them delighted in me or were excited about me. . . . My love for him far exceeds my need for him. Show me the way to love him that is truly good for him, Lord. I stand back now Lord—no more calls, no more letters, always prayer and forgiveness.

Pat still loved her husband, though she described him as unexciting and indifferent. She asked Jesus to help her "to love him as he deserves to be loved." She later wrote, "Please Lord, do not let me hurt or destroy Bob with this—please Lord—don't let me hurt the dearest one in my life." After all, Pat had given birth to four children with Bob, and appreciated his devotion to her. It's just that Frank was so much more exciting. "I loved him so purely at first. I knew he loved me—he saw a piece of my heart and took it as his own. Oh Lord, how we loved in those first years, and you know him, my love, my priest. . . . I treasured our intimate talks, our love words to each other."

Before meeting Frank Flynn, and before her life began to unravel, Pat Hittel had little reason to complain about her situation. She met and fell in love with Bob at age 16, marrying him at 18 while he was in the military. As she would say later, Bob loved her in a quiet way; their life together wasn't thrilling, but Pat was able to stay at home and be a wife and mother—something she felt she was born for. Bob became a building contractor;

they lived comfortably in a bungalow in Fort Lauderdale, and saw their four children grow to be successes. "I had a wonderful mate who adored his children as I did," she recalled. "We were marvelous parents." She realized later, however, that Bob had not loved her "inner life," and then, when a son developed cancer and died, they both plunged into severe depression, unable to help each other. So Pat felt that Frank should have been there, especially then, to comfort her. But he wasn't; he had already found someone else. Nor was he there later when Pat was diagnosed with the cancer that would kill her at age 62.

Believe it not, on the day before she died, Pat gave her last confession to Father Frank and wrote that she had asked the Lord to "forgive us." That was "us," both of them.

When I met Bob, more than a decade after Pat died, he was still grieving, still trying to explain to himself why she had fallen for the priest. He speculated about a psychological concept called transference, which Bob took to mean that Pat had transferred her unconscious love for her father to the priest. Bob also showed me an article in the *Palm Beach Post*, which questioned whether Pat had only dreamed of a physical relationship with Frank, since in her diary entries she did not say explicitly that they had engaged in sex.[5] Was all this just the sexual fantasy of a woman in a mid-life crisis, seeking to break out—at least in her mind—of a restricted existence? Bob didn't buy that explanation, even though it would have been easier on him. Based on what she said in her diary entries—the passionate love for the priest, the trauma over losing him—he had concluded that she was involved with him sexually for a good many years. That view is supported by the fact that Flynn would be accused of sexual misconduct with a girl and with at least six other women. Pat was not his first victim, or his last. The church settled and paid money in three of the cases against him, finally forcing Flynn to resign the priesthood.[6]

Bob told me that he had confronted Flynn three times, and, "each time he jumps up and swears on a bible that there was nothing physical." Flynn later told a newspaper reporter that all he could recall was an occasional

41

hug or kiss between him and Pat, as if there were no blame in a priest kissing a married woman behind her husband's back.[7]

Whatever the relationship, it prompted me to wonder whether America was like a candy store in which priests like Frank Flynn, from the sexually repressed culture of Ireland, could pick and choose the sweets of pretty women like Pat Hittel. As Bob explained to me, "I trusted my wife to him in her struggle for herself and her religion. I feel he took advantage of that and stole my wife's love. . . . He praised her and told her she was beautiful. He became her psychotherapist. As this continued, she fell in love with him and lived for his time with her. His praise and display of love gave her pleasure—she became addicted to this as if she was on dope. She considered her life with me and her family a wasted time." For all that, Bob Hittel says he still deeply loves his late wife, placing on Flynn and the church all the blame for her infatuation over him. Beyond that, he believes that Pat's anxiety over the affair, which she knew was wrong, reduced her immune system and caused the cancer that killed her. When I visited Bob, their home remained a shrine to her, displaying photographs of their 45 years together.

Is Bob a victim? Five years after Pat died, he told me, "I was in such a pitiful state I had to have electric shock treatment. They had to lift me and put me in a wheelchair. I couldn't get out of bed. I was done." Later, he underwent the same treatment again.

I believe that the Hittel case tellingly shows how a priest can abuse a "consenting" woman by listening to her, comforting her, grooming her just as pedophiles have groomed children, intruding on her relationship with her husband, alienating her from him, and then moving on. According to the Hittels, Frank Flynn did just that. Pat wrote that she became an emotional wreck, unable to trust any more priests. Another woman became suicidal after he allegedly seduced her during counseling into having a sexual affair. Others told of unwanted advances; prompting one woman to slap him, hard.[8]

The Flynn case also shows the penchant of Irish priests to protect each other against accusations of wrongdoing. Fr. James Murtagh, interim leader of the Palm Beach diocese during a vacancy in the bishop's office, considered Flynn's involvement with women as "consensual relationships gone sour," as well as unproven. Murtagh promoted Flynn to be a pastor again despite three sex-abuse complaints against him, saying that doctors had cleared Flynn to return after medical treatment.[9] Edward Ricci, a prominent Palm Beach attorney and church benefactor, disagreed, saying Murtagh was helping his longtime friend from Ireland.[10]

I have a special respect for Ed Ricci. He is among committed Catholics who are no longer bowing and kissing the rings of the bishops. I talked to Ricci early on in my investigation of the bishops, and Ed told me about Frank Flynn. He told me about meeting with newly-named Bishop J. Keith Symons to protest the promotion of this predator priest. With Ricci was Michael O'Hara, the psychiatrist for a woman who had become suicidal after allegedly having sex with Flynn. As Ricci remembered the meeting, Symons just sat there without saying a word, and when they finished their presentation he told them, "You are done; you can leave." Murtagh was standing outside chuckling, says Ricci. Symons did nothing.[11]

Seven years later, Symons finally removed Flynn, but only as part of the settlement with another woman who had threatened to sue the church. This woman said Flynn seduced her while her husband was dying of cancer.[12] At that point, Flynn returned to Ireland to work as a volunteer fundraiser at All Hallows College, the seminary that had made him a priest and boasted of its contributions to the American priesthood. Again, Irish Catholic leaders were taking care of their own. By the time Flynn left, eight women had accused him of sexually abusing them—in lawsuits, newspaper interviews and complaints to attorneys, psychiatrists, and church authorities. Did most of the allegations involve just hugs and kisses, which was all Flynn would admit to with Pat Hittel? "He's a liar, a very dishonest man," said psychiatrist O'Hara, who taught a human sexuality course at the Catholic seminary in Palm Beach.[13]

Meantime, the year after Symons expelled Flynn from the ministry, the bishop himself had to resign after admitting he had molested five boys.[14]

Sometimes it takes a novelist to provide historical perspective for the scandals of the times. While investigating the priests from Ireland, I was reading a novel, *Purity of Blood* by Arturo Perez-Reverte, and came across this passage about Spain in the 1600s: "Side by side with unquestionably honorable and saintly clerics, one also found the vile and avaricious: priests who had concubines and bastard children, confessors who preyed on women in the confessional…These scandals were the daily, if not exactly hallowed, bread."[15] Fiction? Not then, as historians confirm, and certainly not now.

If you think Frank Flynn's womanizing was reprehensible, consider Michael Kenny and Paul Cleary. They, too, came from Ireland. According to sworn testimony, Kenny admitted that he had "consensual" sexual intercourse for years with six women and was sexually intimate with four others. One woman, Julia Villegas Phelps, claimed in a lawsuit that he forced himself on her sexually in front of her two small sons when she was not fully conscious because of pain medication. Kenny admitted the sexual encounter but testified the children were asleep in another room. He also admitted he fathered two children by these women, baptizing his own son at the church where he was pastor. The church paid off the mother of his first child.[16]

In writing about these cases, I shake my head in disbelief at the cover-ups and side-stepping of the bishops: their supposed losses of memory, their shucking of responsibility. According to accounts in the *San Antonio Express-News*, Kenny told Archbishop Patrick Flores early on about his philandering, but Flores didn't want to know about it. Flores claimed he didn't learn about Kenny's sexual involvements until seven years later, when a long-time church secretary complained he seduced her as a teenager. Besides, said the archbishop, the sex was consensual and the actions of the women were partly responsible for their claimed loss of faith. "Sin always affects our faith, and they were sinning for all those years," Flores was quoted as saying. "They are not babies. Why didn't they tell us about it when it happened?" Why didn't they? J. Douglas Sutter, attorney for Phelps, answered: "She feared for the well-being of her children if this got out.

Father Kenny even told her that if it gets out, what's been going on, that it would be really bad for her and her children." The church eventually suspended Kenny and settled the Phelps lawsuit for $300,000. As could be expected, Kenny flew back to Ireland to join the many other errant priests from America.[17]

Even then, the San Antonio archdiocese refused to admit that Kenny was at fault. They only settled the Phelps case, a church official said, because a trial would have hurt the church, Catholics in general and, yes, the alleged victim and her family. "We believe we could have won this case," Monsignor Lawrence Stuebben said. "But it would have been a bruising and hurtful trial to the individuals involved." He spoke with authority as the vicar general, second in command of the San Antonio church. Could there have been another reason? It seems that there was. The settlement saved the church from damaging public testimony by Kenny that would have cast doubt on the archbishop's claims he knew nothing about the priest's sexual activities. That was the view of attorney Sutter, and it sounds more plausible than the church version.[18]

When I say some bishops would take no responsibility for the abuses of their priests, I offer again Archbishop Flores as a prime example in another case, this one involving Fr. Paul Cleary. In a letter, Flores brushed off a woman who had complained about Cleary. "Personally," he wrote, "I believe that if Fr. Paul Cleary inflicted pain in you, it is up to him to help you find psychological and medical relief. I don't believe the rest of the archdiocese should be punished for something that an individual does improperly." That was a bit curt, but maybe the victim was somewhat mollified by his closing comment, "I will keep you, your family, and your intentions in my daily prayers and I ask to be remembered in yours. . . Sincerely in the Lord." The offending "individual," of course, was one of the priests Flores had appointed to the woman's parish.[19]

That woman had written to express hurt and dismay over the fact that Cleary was still a pastor in a position to abuse vulnerable women. As she explained it, Cleary had encouraged her to establish a relationship with him as she sought help in dealing with a husband who was physically and emotionally abusive, as well as unfaithful. She conceded that she had developed strong feelings for Cleary at first; he was kind, gentle and supportive. But then she began to feel uncomfortable, as if she had gone from one bad relationship to another. All she asked from Flores was for him to pay for counseling for up to a year to help her deal not only with a divorce "but with deception, betrayal and abuse by a counselor, a priest." She did not sue to seek lots of money, the motive church officials often attribute to abuse victims.[20]

The archbishop finally compelled Cleary to pay for counseling, though for no more than one year. When the year was almost up, Flores wrote the counseling service to say that, "after thoughtful consideration, prayer and consultation," he decided there would be no more payments. It was only a few thousand dollars, and even then Cleary was way behind in paying. I would suggest that the archbishop, as a showing of good will, could have paid for the continued counseling for the pain his priest allegedly had inflicted on the victim.[21]

Up to that point, the charming priest from Ireland had been able to have his way with women—four of them—with impunity. First, there was talk that he had to leave one parish because he was responsible for the breakup of a marriage. Then, there was the woman who visited him frequently late at night in the parish residence, whereupon they would go to his bedroom and close the door. She was followed by a young woman who said she had a "relationship" with Cleary and felt he was abandoning her for someone else. That relationship also had started when the woman, a minor at the time, was receiving counseling—this one for being sexually abused by her parents. Like Kenny, Cleary waited until the girl was 18 before having sexual relations with her. The allegations are credible. They were partly confirmed by Monsignor Patrick Walsh, his supervising pastor at Holy Spirit parish in San Antonio, and by the church's insurance company. In fact, the company excluded Cleary from future coverage because of his sexual misconduct.[22] (The church has reported that in each of the past four years, insurance has covered from 27 to 49 percent of the cost of abuse settlements, including coverage of more than one-third of the record $660 million Los Angeles settlement.) Cleary declined comment.

Cleary wound up leaving Holy Spirit parish in the wake of the sexual allegations. However, Walsh said that Cleary left not because he was responsible for breaking up a marriage, but because he was eligible for his own parish. There's no way to know, but perhaps Cleary was promoted to run his own parish precisely because of his charming appeal.

Jane Reasor described his charm when he arrived as pastor at St. Dominic Catholic Church, dressed like a Texas cowboy. Reasor, then the church receptionist, recalled that he had a "fantastic personality," and many female admirers. As one of his admirers, Reasor said, she developed a long-term relationship that included gambling trips to Las Vegas. But in this case, contrary to the others, the priest could have been the victim of the woman, showing the risk for clerics involved in such relationships. When Reasor, as office manager, was accused of stealing money from the church, she claimed that Cleary, with his history of female involvements, had set her up to cover his own skimming of parish funds. A judge didn't buy it and a federal prosecutor rejected her claim of a "romantic" liaison. She pled guilty to embezzling more than $470,000 from the church, was sentenced to three years in prison, and ordered to repay the money.[23]

Most often, as I have noted in case after case, the adult woman is ultimately the victim, even if she consented at first—usually during counseling—to a romantic relationship with her priest. But the church does not always see it that way. In reference to the Cleary case, for example, an attorney for the Catholic Mutual Group insurance firm said that the church has been relatively successful in defending itself in "consenting adults" cases.[24] But even if the sex is honestly consensual, the priest is violating his vow of celibacy, which, according to Fr. Augustine Sheehan, is "wrong, really, but it happens." Sheehan, a native of Ireland, was accused of rape by a former nun, also from Ireland. He said it was consensual.[25]

The Catholic Church and its agents allowed the three Irish priests,

Flynn, Kenny and Cleary, to remain in active ministry for years despite their involvements with women. Walsh, another priest of Irish ancestry, told Cleary to stop taking women into his bedroom, but did nothing to stop Cleary from starting a relationship with a minor who had been sexually abused by her parents.[26] I can't generalize from these cases to say that the church often goes easy on celibacy violations when the participants are adults. I also don't have enough information either to say that church-men from Ireland or of Irish descent often protect their own kind from punishment. But is logical to assume that church authorities, many of whom have been sexually involved themselves, would be reluctant to remove priests who dally with women. To do so would seriously deplete the ranks of the clergy, considering estimates that up to half of priests have violated their celibacy vows. Perhaps the Vatican won't discuss repealing the celibacy rule because an open debate would reveal how widely it is ignored already and cause more priests to leave.

Elimination of the celibacy requirement might retain those who would otherwise leave in order to marry, but it would not stop predators, like these three Irish priests, from chasing and victimizing women.

CHAPTER FOUR

THE BISHOP
AND THE BOYS

I N MY QUEST IN IRELAND for clues as to what turned favorite son
Anthony O'Connell into a sexual predator, I started with family and
friends, then went to his schools. Did he have an unhappy home life? Was
he sexually repressed or confused as an adolescent? Was he sexually abused
or sexually involved at school? Or was he just a normal Irish lad, living a
normal life in a large family, showing no signs of sexual problems?

Maybe I was naïve to think I could get people to answer such questions. Yet, I hoped that the Irish would be open, friendly, and talkative, true
to well-worn stereotypes. At least, I thought they'd want to tell me about
the goodness of their native son, to counter the dark side portrayed in the
news media.

Naïve or not, that's what I expected when I met O'Connell's brother-
in-law, John McNamara, at the family home near Ballynacally, a tiny community with a convenience store, pub and church, south of the lovely town
of Ennis in County Clare, in delightful western Ireland. I introduced myself as a journalist from the United States, stated the purpose of my visit
and asked if I could speak to his wife, the bishop's sister. No, he said; she
was not there and wouldn't be there for me. He then asked me to leave,
saying he was busy and didn't want to talk.

Anticipating the Irish to be a direct people, I was not taken aback at his abrupt dismissal. As he saw me to my car, he asked what I was going to write. I told him I was planning to write about the sexual involvements of Catholic bishops like his brother-in-law, but was particularly interested in learning more about the life of Anthony O'Connell.

Anthony never abused anyone, McNamara said. He never admitted to any abuse, and the courts had cleared him. Take that back to your newspaper, he added. At that point, he again ordered me to leave his property.

Not one to give up easily, I went a few days later to see O'Connell's foster brother, Joe McCarthy. According to this family member, brother Anthony was the nicest individual you ever met. A very holy man. A very religious hard-working man.

Just when I thought McCarthy would be open to conversation, he shut down. Suspicious that I wouldn't write about all the good things his brother did, McCarthy decided it was better to tell me nothing, one way or the other. He told me to have a nice stay in Ireland and ended the interview.

Brother Gus O'Connell was the exception in the family. He talked to me twice by telephone from his home in Dublin, across the island from Ballynacally. He's not sure Anthony was guilty of any abuse. The media use that term, he said, but look at what Anthony actually said—inappropriate touching of two teenagers while lying in bed. That is not abuse. Anthony had called it an experimental approach to therapy.

Looking back, said Gus, it was foolish of Anthony, but not abusive. I asked Gus about the later allegations of abuse by seven other young men. He didn't believe them. I then asked about the "love" letters Anthony exchanged with two young men. Gus had no comment on those.[1]

I don't want to be overly critical of the O'Connell family. What family doesn't rally to the support of a son or brother who gets in trouble, especially when he has risen in America to the exalted position of bishop? And they didn't have a lot of information; just what Anthony told them and an article in their local newspaper. But the newspaper article was enough to put the lie to the bishop's benign initial account, issued on the day he resigned, of his contact with one of the young men. Actually, they were both naked in bed. O'Connell claimed he was a do-gooder, trying through therapy to help the teenager come to terms with his body. Help? In bed, naked? Well, that's what he said, and that's what his family believed, or said they believed. After all, as the bishop said, he had not engaged in sexual activity as such and didn't view his conduct at the time as sexual abuse.[2]

But it was all part of the big lie. Much, much more would come out later about the prelate of Palm Beach, Florida, and his long-standing attraction to male students when he was a priest on the staff and later director of a Missouri seminary, and then as bishop. Other alleged victims came forward until the total reached nine. Some of the young men, including three who were minors when allegedly first abused, were gay or confused about their sexual orientation. They told of masturbation, of sleeping together naked with O'Connell rubbing his body against theirs, of an attempt at oral sex and other sexual contact, continuing in at least one case for more than 20 years. The bishop said it was therapy.

O'Connell carried on these alleged sexual relationships for more than a quarter of a century, from shortly after he joined the staff at the Hannibal, Missouri, seminary in the mid-1960s through his time as bishop in Knoxville, Tennessee. More recently, until just before he resigned in 2002, he had made more than $30,000 in regular payments to two of the young men. Even after he resigned, he pleaded with one long-time sexual companion, "with the love of God," to keep from going public in a lawsuit, offering to help him the rest of his life.[3]

How and why did the bishop and his victims keep secret his abuse for so long? "He had a masterful way of seducing people and endearing people to him; it was the way he maintained secrecy," said Christopher Dixon, who, at age 13, was molested by O'Connell in the seminary and later was paid $125,000 by the church in a secret agreement for the abuse at the hands of O'Connell and two other priests. This endearment prompted some of his victims to continue their sexual relationships with O'Connell long after they were first abused.[4]

Stunningly, in the mid-1990s, before O'Connell was assigned to the Palm Beach diocese, three bishops had learned about his sexual involvements but kept them secret. One was Bishop Michael McAuliffe, a close friend who had attended a celebration for O'Connell in Ireland when he first became a bishop at Knoxville in 1988. McAuliffe, now deceased, had been O'Connell's boss in Jefferson City for two decades, and as bishop agreed to the secret settlement with Dixon, one of O'Connell's first victims. The other bishops were John Gaydos, who followed McAuliffe in Jefferson City, and Raymond Boland of Kansas City-St. Joseph, who, like O'Connell, came from Ireland and by his silence was protecting his own kind.

Because of the Irish connection, I consider Bishop Boland's involvement of particular interest in this narrative. Boland was first brought into the case by another O'Connell victim, when he was interviewed by attorney Anderson for a lawsuit. In that interview, and by Anderson's account later, the young man (who has asked to remain anonymous) said he approached Boland after mass one day, set up an appointment in the bishop's office, and told him about the abuse, but said he wanted to keep it quiet. Boland was more than happy to oblige, saying "that's the way we like to handle it." Through a spokesman later, Boland said he could not recall any such conversation and, moreover, was out of the office that day. Tellingly, the victim had not talked of any specific day. And when Boland was asked about it by another reporter more than two years later, he backed off a bit; said nothing about being out of the office, admitted a "layman" had inquired about O'Connell's whereabouts, but again denied that he discussed any abuse allegations with this layman. Another lying bishop? Or had the "layman" made it all up—in considerable detail? I have little doubt about who was telling the truth.[5]

McAuliffe also knew about O'Connell's sexual misconduct because Dixon had told him about it and the bishop had approved the Dixon settlement. "I informed McAuliffe about O'Connell and the other two priests," Dixon told me. "He assured me he was going to deal with it and take care of the problem." McAuliffe took care of the problem by keeping it a secret.

If McAuliffe and the other bishops had alerted the Vatican of the O'Connell problem, as they should have done, the Irish bishop probably would have been forced to resign much earlier, the pope would not have assigned him to Palm Beach, and the church would have avoided a huge embarrassment. He had been sent there to restore respect after the resignation of Bishop Symons for multiple sexual abuse. The Symons-O'Connell debacle produced two strikes against the church, thanks to the culture of secrecy that so often makes accountability an alien concept. One prominent bishop, however, did not condone the secrecy. In a rare showing of hierarchical outrage, Bishop Wilton Gregory, then head of the U.S. Conference of Catholic Bishops, said that the failure of Jefferson City Catholic officials to tell the Vatican about O'Connell's abuse was a "travesty."[6] That's a strong word, well applied.

I didn't expect the people in Ireland to know the details of their bishop's demise, but I hoped they might shed light on what in his background might have caused O'Connell to seek the illicit homosexual relationships that destroyed his career in the United States. I consider O'Connell particularly important to my story because he is the most prominent same-sex abuser among the priests exported from Ireland to the States. I found in my research that, while an unusually high percentage of the Irish priests molested girls, about half preyed on boys or young men, as did O'Connell.

Who really is this man who fell so far into disgrace? To know O'Connell the man, I thought it important to know Anthony the child and adolescent. Flann Neylon, who sang a school song at the hometown celebration for the new bishop, counts himself as one of O'Connell's best childhood friends. They went together to primary school up the hill, hit the picture shows on Sundays, competed in hurling and football, hung out at Neylon's house, got together when Tony came home on holidays from secondary school in the city of Cork. According to Flann, neither he nor O'Connell had girlfriends; not because such relationships were discouraged in a sexually repressive culture, but because they had no interest in girls and no time for them. Neylon agreed with brother Gus that O'Connell was a socially outgoing young man, even if he developed relationships only with those of his own sex. As for Neylon, a retired farmer, he went on to marry and raise two children.

Neylon disagreed with Gus, however, on how O'Connell decided to be a priest. According to Gus, his brother felt he had a calling to be a religious brother while he was in primary school, went to secondary school run by the Presentation Brothers in Cork, and then changed his mind, left that school and decided to pursue a priestly career. Neylon said his friend didn't want to be a priest, really wanted to stay home and enjoy himself, but was forced by his mother to be a man of God. "She told him all the time, 'Go back to school and be a priest,'" Neylon remembered. "Everybody wanted a son to be a priest." Why didn't Anthony want to be a priest? "I think he thought it was tough in school . . . and maybe he felt he was not as good as the others." Nevertheless, he followed his mother's wishes, finished at secondary school in Ennis, run by the Christian Brothers, and went on to study philosophy for two years at Mungret College under the Jesuits.[7]

I should note that the Christian Brothers were the worst offenders in a horrible epidemic of sexual and physical abuse that continued for decades at their boarding schools in Ireland.[8] As at Mungret, however, I found no evidence that O'Connell was a victim or perpetrator of abuse at the Christian Brothers boarding school in Ennis, where he was a day student, not a boarder.

Before O'Connell left for America, something happened that almost derailed his career. It must have happened at the Mungret College in Limerick, where the young man from Ballynacally was on the track to be a priest. The Catholic bishop of Birmingham was paying for his Mungret studies and would bring him to the states for seminary training to make him a man of God in Alabama. But then the Alabama diocese dropped him and O'Connell—who came from a family of limited means in a country of endemic poverty—had to find another American bishop who would pay the rest of his way to the priesthood.[9]

Getting another sponsor should have been easy at a time when bishops all over the United States were recruiting Irish priests to serve their expanding flocks of believers. Some of the recruiters were going to Mungret, promising God and mammon, or material as well as spiritual benefits in their territories. Some of Mungret students, rightly pleading poverty in an impoverished country, would go to what they called the "dollar diocese" in Alabama, so named because of the $20 to $25 in dollar bills they would get with Christmas cards. Many students also went to work for other bishops who were prepared to "hand out money left, right, and center," recalled former Mungret teacher Donal Gannon. As part of their appeal, the bishops would take groups of Mungret students out to dinner in Limerick. These prelates were like college recruiters offering incentives to lure the most talented football or basketball players for their teams. But O'Connell was not one of the chosen ones. As I have noted, after Alabama rejected him and he went job-hunting, 36 bishops and abbots turned him down before the small, newly formed Jefferson City diocese in Missouri took a chance on him, paying for four years of seminary training and ordaining him to be a priest—eventually to its regret.[10]

I went to Limerick to ask the Jesuits what happened at Mungret to turn their student O'Connell into a pariah as a candidate for the priesthood. Unfortunately, the Mungret authorities who would have known why he was rejected are now deceased. His former classmates, whom I tracked down by telephone all over Ireland and America, said they had no idea what happened to "Tony." And O'Connell, having retreated to a monastery after resigning, was not granting interviews.

From an authoritative account in a Ballynacally-Lissycasey parish publication, however, I concluded that the Jesuits had found O'Connell unfit to be a priest, or putting it more gently, they found that he didn't have a vocation to represent God. From this, I figured that Fr. Brendan Barry, a tough-minded reformer at Mungret who was cleaning out unfit candidates for the priesthood, must have passed this conclusion on to the bishops who asked about him. Frank O'Neill, a Jesuit priest sharing tea and cookies with me in Limerick, agreed with that conclusion. "Was O'Connell blackballed?" I asked. Obviously he was, O'Neill answered. The Mungret authorities, including Barry, did what they had to do, O'Neill said: they told the truth about O'Connell to the American bishops. O'Neill had gone to Mungret before O'Connell and was head of the Jesuit community in Limerick when I talked to him. As for Mungret, it had been closed for many years over lack of students. There would be no more recruits from there.[11]

Still looking for answers. I followed O'Neill's suggestion that I talk to Joseph Brennan, who was a teacher at Mungret while O'Connell was there. As Brennan remembered it, college president Barry was "ruthless" in dealing with families he felt were getting the American bishops to pay for the education of their sons, assuring them of free tickets to the states, where they would abandon the priesthood and go on to other careers. "He cleared a lot of guys out," Brennan said. So if Barry had any doubts about O'Connell, for whatever reason, Brennan said, he would "in justice" have let the American bishops know about his concerns.

I wondered whether O'Connell had been blackballed because he was involved in sexual activity at Mungret, as a precursor to his later misconduct. Neither O'Neill nor Brennan knew about that, though Brennan thought it was unlikely. Nonetheless, former student Martin Igoe and teachers Brennan and Gannon suggested the possibilities of such activity. They remembered students telling each other to avoid a certain teacher who invited some into his room after showers—a teacher suddenly removed from the faculty; another teacher preferring the company of young students; a student Gannon saw bending over the knee of Mungret's Dan McDonald. Brennan added that McDonald, a priest, scholar and head of the college before Barry, "may have had an interest in smaller boys."[12] O'Connell, who was an older, not smaller, student, would name that now deceased official as one of his mentors. But O'Connell was not implicated in any of this talk; on the contrary he was described as stable, conscientious, and a hard worker.

For all the talk of sexual possibilities, no one had heard about or seen any overt sexual activity. I asked Gannon, however, whether it was unusual for a student to be on the lap of a Mungret priest. "It might be he was pitying a kid who was lonely or upset," he said. "It's hard to think it was sexual." Actually, after having read about so many cases of clergy misconduct, I didn't find it hard at all to believe it could have been sexual. An adult doesn't ordinarily have a teenager leaning over his lap. (I say that as a father of eight children, including five teenagers at one time.)

Of course, O'Connell could have been blackballed for other reasons. Gannon thought maybe he didn't show an inclination to be a priest—didn't show kindness, was boastful, puffed up about himself. Yet, according to colleagues, O'Connell did not display these deficiencies as a priest. O'Neill suggested that maybe O'Connell wasn't prayerful enough to be a priest. The old Jesuit was as forthcoming and helpful as he could be, even digging up Mungret yearbooks of the late 1950s showing O'Connell with his classmates at the time. Later, I talked to many of them. They said he never told them why he was turned down so often; one remembered that he was quite upset about losing Alabama as a sponsor. Most, like Brennan and Igoe, were still priests when I talked to them; Gannon was not.

The problem was that Father Barry, who would know, had died long ago, and there was no paper trail shedding light on the bishop's early college problems, if any. Father Fergus O'Donoghue, who maintained the Jesuit archives in Dublin, told me that the Mungret records did not show whether O'Connell had been rejected because of unsatisfactory grades or personal factors. "The records . . . contain no references to the character of any of the students," he said.[13]

That was it, period. After all this fruitless research, I was left with these nagging questions: Where, when, and why did Anthony O'Connell develop the propensity, as priest and bishop, to engage in homosexual sex with boys and young men? Had he been sexually involved with a student or priest at Mungret College, prior to arrival in America in his early 20s?

In my continuing search for answers, I considered another possibility: that O'Connell himself might have been abused as a child or young man, thus causing him to be an abuser. Remember, pedophile Oliver O'Grady had been molested by a brother and two priests as a youth in Ireland, had himself abused his little sister and allegedly turned to abusing other boys before he became a predator priest in America.[14] I wondered whether early abuse had led O'Connell to engage in sexual activity at Mungret College, putting his career in jeopardy. Indeed, the study on clergy sexual abuse of children, prepared for the American bishops and released in 2004, found that some priests accused of abuse had themselves previously been molested, though the actual number was unknown. [15]

I was not the first to raise this question about O'Connell. Attorney Jeffrey Anderson asked the bishop in a deposition in 2003, "Bishop O'Connell, have you, at any time, been sexually molested or abused?" O'Connell's attorney responded, "I'm going to object on the grounds that the question is far afield from any relevant issue in the case and not within the bounds of discovery and also advise the witness that he can assert his privilege against self-incrimination in response to that question." Accordingly, the bishop declined to answer.[16]

I asked Anderson later if, in taking O'Connell's deposition for an abuse lawsuit, he had any information indicating that O'Connell had been abused. He said the question was based only on intuition. I would say, however, that he had good reasons for asking it, considering that he probably knows more about clergy sex abuse than any other attorney in the country, having handled hundreds of lawsuits for victims. I give Anderson and other attorneys a lot of credit for taking sex abuse out of the secret files of the Catholic Church and showing it to be a huge problem the church could no longer suppress. Sure, as critics say, some of the attorneys have made a lot of money taking on the church, but this threat to its finances helped prompt the church to address the problem. And some of the attorneys spent a lot of money on costly lawsuits for little or no return, as in the O'Connell case, for reasons I will explain later.

As for O'Connell, it appears that only he can answer the question of how or why he became the child abuser he was. And he isn't talking. Others

I talked to, including childhood friend Flann Neylon, said they didn't know the answer. His brother, Gus, also said that if Anthony was ever abused, he wasn't aware of it. The bishop is keeping the secret as he helps Trappist monks in a large chicken ranch at the Mepkin monastery in South Carolina.

When I went to the monastery to interview O'Connell, I was told falsely that he wasn't there. An enterprising reporter for the *Palm Beach Post* finally found him by going to Mepkin to participate in a religious retreat for people seeking inner peace and spiritual renewal. There was O'Connell, whose spiritual life had been shattered, reading from scripture and, wearing his priestly vestments, helping celebrate mass.[17]

O'Connell fits the profile of other American bishops, Irish or not, accused of abusing children and adults. For many years they kept their sinful secrets, advancing their careers while enjoying the protection of their fellow bishops. When they were publicly exposed, they quickly resigned and went into seclusion, in monasteries or convents, seldom to be heard from again. In contrast, consider that more than 100 errant priests, like Oliver O'Grady, have gone to prison, and many more have been defrocked or removed from the priesthood.[18] But not one American bishop in recent history has been defrocked or spent any time behind bars. They have been coddled.

Although he sleeps in a relatively small monastic cell, O'Connell is no prisoner. He has traveled back to Ireland to visit family and friends. His brother Gus, once a missionary religious brother in Africa, now married and living in Dublin, regularly talks to the bishop by phone and says, "He is following the monastery life and is very happy with it. He intends to stay there."

If he is happy, as his brother says, he has reason to be so. If O'Connell and other bishops had been prosecuted, they might not have fared so well. Many of them were guilty not only of criminal abuse themselves, but also covered up, or aided and abetted, the criminal abuses of their priests. O'Connell, for example, while bishop in Palm Beach, made it possible for Father Matthew Fitzgerald, also from Ireland, to retain his priestly duties despite allegations that he had repeatedly molested teenage boys and young men.[19] I think it's fair to say that the bishop's ability to deal with such cases was compromised by his own criminal abuses.

In my investigation of the hierarchy in North America and Europe, I found that more than 60 bishops and abbots had been accused of sexual involvements with children and adults. But of all those, often involving alleged criminal behavior, only one had gone to prison—Irishman Hubert O'Connor of British Columbia in Canada. O'Connor served six months behind bars on a conviction of raping a young native woman at a boarding school. But then the conviction was overturned on a technicality and O'Connor went free—to live in a convent, of course. I should note that O'Connor did talk to me, denying that he had sex with the young woman the night after he was made bishop. An isolated case? In early 2006 it was reported that the Canadian government and several church organizations agreed to pay nearly $2 billion to native people to settle claims of sexual and physical abuse in those residential schools, financed by the government and run by the churches, including the Catholic Church.[20] It should be no surprise that some of the Canadian abusers came from Ireland.

While provincial authorities went after O'Connor in Canada, local prosecutors in America didn't bring any criminal charges against Symons and O'Connell. It was easy for police and prosecutors to assign the two cases to their files because, as a result of prolonged cover-up, they hadn't known about the alleged crimes until decades later, when the statute of limitations appeared to have run out. So when attorney Anderson asked O'Connell in his deposition if criminal authorities had made any attempt to investigate him, the bishop could truthfully say, "I'm not aware of any." Two years later, however, the courts ruled in a case involving a priest that there were no time limits for prosecuting rape and sodomy cases. That ruling would have made it possible for a case to be brought against the bishop for attempted sodomy, as alleged by one of his victims. Or an aggressive prosecutor might have pursued the case anyway, as did the prosecutor in St. Louis who won the favorable ruling that involved a priest.

There was no aggressive prosecutor, however, willing to take on either of the two bishops.

Until recent years, I suspect that many law enforcement authorities in this country have been reluctant to risk the possible political consequences of taking on the Catholic Church and its bishops. Indeed, in heavily Catholic southern Louisiana, prosecutor Doug Greenburg lost reelection after obtaining a life sentence for a priest accused of rape. At one point, when Greenburg had threatened to ask the court to hold the local bishop in contempt of court, he was accused of putting the Catholic Church on trial.[21]

In another case in Spokane, Washington, authorities were complicit with church officials in covering up serious criminal allegations against a bishop. They buried in their files allegations that Irish-American Bishop Lawrence Welsh in 1986 had tried to strangle a young male prostitute while seeking oral sex. As in the O'Connell case, three bishops were involved in the cover-up. When Welsh resigned, he was transferred to the Twin Cities in Minnesota, where he served as an auxiliary bishop under the protection of his friend, the late Irish-American Archbishop Roach.[22]

Aside from the inclination of the Irish bishops to protect each other, which I discuss elsewhere in this book, I submit that there is another point to be made in the Roach-Welsh relationship. The point is that because of their vow of celibacy, the prelates are often compelled to do whatever is necessary, even to lie at times, to cover up their own intimate relationships with other men or women, even of the most benign kind. Welsh admitted an egregious sexual sin. Roach, on the other hand, merely had a close relationship with a woman in a small town south of Minneapolis, Minnesota. In that case, there was talk about the archbishop, who at the time had alcohol problems, coming down regularly to see her or attend her parties; even showing up drunk once at her office. There was more talk when a cleaning woman mentioned seeing his clothes in a closet of her home. When I asked him about all this, Roach said that he and the woman were good friends, but sex was not part of it. As for the clothes, he said he thought they were in her home because the two of them had gone on a couple of Wisconsin "trips," a word he quickly changed to a less incriminating "excursions." The relationship came to an end when she committed suicide for unknown reasons. The archbishop presided at her funeral service and later would become the prestigious president of the National Conference of Catholic Bishops.

As I mentioned earlier, O'Connell hid his sexual transgressions for more than two decades. When finally caught, he avoided any jail time, but he and the church still faced civil lawsuits seeking damages for the abuses. There again, however, he got off easy. Two suits were settled for token amounts and the remaining three were dismissed—again for having been filed too late. O'Connell was off the hook, for good. As was the church.

But is O'Connell really off the hook? This is the man who will pay the rest of his life for his sexual compulsions, the man who had risen from a poor Irish family to one of the most powerful positions in the Catholic Church, the man who had been honored in his hometown as a conquering hero when he became bishop, the man who traveled the world on church missions. And then to be working on a monastery chicken farm, where animal rights advocates recently accused the monks of mistreating, not children, but chickens (an allegation the abbot vehemently denied). Oh my, how the world turns, as do the fortunes of men.

As I found in Ireland, O'Connell's friends, relatives, and fellow priests still think of him as a wonderful person. They described him to me as a nice boy, a nice man, knowledgeable, studious, brainy, popular, affable, a solid citizen, leader, down to earth, kind, jolly, chirpy, unpretentious, warm, uncomplicated, countryish. When he came home for the holidays, they recall, he gave sermons about getting along with neighbors. Some say he was unfairly accused. Others say he is human and humans are weak, a rationale often used to justify all kinds of aberrant behavior, though priests are supposed to be morally better than other humans. One acquaintance, who asked that his name not be used, was realistic about him: "I'm not bitter but he let the people down."

Perhaps the best epitaph for the career of Anthony O'Connell can be found up a winding road near his family home. That's where you come upon his two-room primary school building, abandoned and in ruins, windows broken, doors padlocked, surrounded by impenetrable blackberry bushes. Down below, at his family church, on a cold, dark rainy Sunday, people continue in the practice of their faith at 10 o'clock mass, the priest in his sermon lamenting evil, calling for peace, joy and gentleness. After mass, two old-timers remember O'Connell as a friendly boy.

It all seemed so far removed from the headline in the British tabloid, *The Sun*: "Perv Bishop 'Sorry' for Romp with Boy."

CHAPTER FIVE

GAY BOYS

A S EARLY AS AGE 9 or 10, Matthew Cosby knew that he was "different" from other boys his age. By the time he was 12, he was sure that
he was homosexual, or "gay" as he would come to describe himself.[1] As an
adult, he said, "That was not, is not my choice. I am gay and although at
times it is painful, I am happy. I accept this part of me just as I accept my
hair, my body, my personality, I accept it and I rejoice in it."[2]

Cosby accepted himself for who he was, but he did not accept the way
his Catholic Church viewed him. "I'm angry because the church and the
world seem to reject me for a part of who I am," he said. "I did not choose
homosexuality, I did not. And yet I am condemned."[3] I read Cosby's profound testimonial in a sexual-abuse lawsuit and wondered whether that
church, speaking through the Godlike voice of the Vatican, had fully considered Catholics like Matthew Cosby when it proclaimed gays to be victims of an objective, intrinsic "disorder" and in 2005 renewed efforts to
keep them out of the priesthood.[4]

Cosby's sexual orientation, however it was viewed, had not kept him as
a teenager from wanting to be a priest. He enrolled in the St. Thomas
Aquinas high school seminary in Hannibal, Missouri, to begin studies for
the priesthood. And that's where his troubles began, not only because he was
gay, but because the head of the seminary, Anthony O'Connell from Ireland, lured him into a sexual relationship that lasted for eight years. At first,

Cosby thought he was special to the popular priest (soon to be a bishop), but he later learned that O'Connell had many other "special" boys at the seminary. Then he became very angry, both at O'Connell and the church.

He had a right to be angry. Before prominent Catholic leaders began blaming homosexual priests for the sex-abuse crisis in their church, priest O'Connell was exploiting gay and sexually confused boys and young men for his sexual pleasure, over a period of 24 years.[5] In his case, we see a stark example of how the church deals with one of the most difficult and explosive issues of modern times: homosexuality within the ranks of the priesthood. How do church authorities respond? By saying one thing and doing another, depending on the status of those involved in the homosexual practices they consider seriously sinful.

While church authorities barred from the priesthood three victims of O'Connell's abuse because of their homosexual desires and behavior, three bishops covered up O'Connell's own homosexual activity to save his career as bishop.[6] Indeed, O'Connell was directly involved in the decision to deny the priesthood to one of his victims.[7]

Just as I have described the complex personalities of other priests in this narrative, however, Anthony O'Connell was not some one-dimensional monster preying on children. In fact, in a good sense, he had a special way with the teenage boys at St. Thomas Aquinas, where he was a teacher and later the director. He related to them as a friend, teased them, played with them, and sympathized with them. As one put it, he was like a father. They admired, even loved him. But soon after he arrived at the seminary, he also gave way to his compulsions, started abusing them sexually, individually and privately, going from one to another, sometimes more than one at a time, molesting them even after he became bishop in Knoxville, Tennessee. The best count is that he initiated at least nine homosexual relationships at the seminary. The bishop has never said whether he considers himself a homosexual, or whether he just acted that way all those years, engaging in same-sex activity from prolonged fondling and mutual masturbation to naked body-rubbing.[8]

The difference between the bishop and the young men is that he got away with his homosexual activity within the clergy for a long time, while, as I mentioned, three of his victims never made it to the priesthood. Church authorities dashed the clerical dreams of Cosby and Tom Lindsay—a pseudonym for another O'Connell victim. The third, Michael Wegs, said he was ousted because his bishop, Michael McAuliffe, considered him to be a promiscuous homosexual "pervert."[9]

McAuliffe apparently didn't know that Christopher Dixon, also an O'Connell victim at the seminary, had sex with other students. Dixon was able to continue his studies to become a priest, then finally blew the whistle on the Irish bishop and left the priesthood in disgust. Whom did Dixon tell about O'Connell's misconduct? Well, Bishop McAuliffe, of course. And who kept it a secret to protect Bishop O'Connell? Yes, McAuliffe.[10]

Lindsay was particularly bitter about the duplicity of his church in its treatment of homosexuals. "What about those of us who were kicked out of seminary for being honest about our feelings?" he asked O'Connell in an e-mail message before the bishop resigned.[11] Lindsay added later, "I feel that I was called (to the priesthood) but then denied. It really hurts."[12] It may have hurt Lindsay, but it apparently didn't bother O'Connell too much. The record of his case indicates that he did little or nothing to defend his students when they were barred from the priesthood—he was not about to put his career in jeopardy. His students were expendable. In fact, after Lindsay spent months confiding with O'Connell about his sexual attraction to other male students, O'Connell and the head of the seminary "told him they thought he probably should leave." He did. Even then, Lindsay was able to get into another seminary later, but then left for good.[13] His urge to be a priest had been obviously strong, despite the many years of sexual misconduct by O'Connell, the priest who should have been setting an example for him.

Cosby also had been honest about his feelings—and sexual behavior. He had decided to leave the Kenrick seminary in Saint Louis because he didn't believe in celibacy and wanted to live a gay lifestyle. But a month later, he changed his mind and asked to continue his studies. "I was asked not to return," he said. By then, Cosby would admit later, he had been sexually involved with seven males. Though that sounds like a lot, it isn't as many as O'Connell was accused of sexually abusing. O'Connell, who ironically also had studied at Kenrick, stayed on as a bishop.

I sought to examine the bishop's relationships with these four young men—Cosby, Lindsay, Wegs and Dixon—because I wanted to learn, from their experiences and in their words, how this man from Ireland could have been sexually involved with them for so long without anyone complaining. Consider his sporadic relationship with Lindsay over 24 years; how was that kept quiet? I think part of the answer is that, at the time, as boys they didn't feel that their sexual encounters with O'Connell were abusive. According to them, each felt he was special to the priest, and naively accepted his sexual advances as attempts to help them deal with their own sexual problems and other personal difficulties. Beyond that, the question would be why three of the boys, Dixon, Cosby, and Lindsay, allowed the relationships to continue well into adulthood. The answer to that appears to be that they had already engaged in sex with other boys, and didn't consider it unusual to continue doing so with adult O'Connell.

The fact is, they accepted him because he accepted them, as homosexual boys all. He made that clear in an e-mail message to Lindsay: "You're right—people in the church have been slow in learning to understand the whole question on homosexuality and in knowing how to deal with persons in a sensitive, compassionate, Christian fashion. I am very sorry that you had to suffer so much. I have rejoiced every time you have taken steps forward, when your spiritual life has perked up and taken off, as in your recent exciting pilgrimage to Rome. . . . With prayers and love, O'C."[14]

I suggest that O'Connell understood them because he was one of them, acting out of a powerful compulsion to engage in homosexual behavior, the very behavior the Catholic Church is trying to eliminate from the priesthood. O'Connell also appealed to them because of his Irish charm, which overcame his lack of any physical attraction. He was a stout man with a bulbous nose, as Wegs described him. Maybe because of that Irish charm, he was highly successful in recruiting young men for the Hannibal seminary, including Cosby and Lindsay. Did he sense even then that they might be objects of his sexual desires? I doubt it. Or was he deluded into thinking he really was trying to help them, and really wasn't doing anything seriously wrong? He may have thought so at first, though this is debatable. As I noted earlier, an adult lying naked in bed with a boy stretches the definition of therapy. And he certainly wasn't "helping" them as adults.

Even then, it would be easy in this narrative to portray O'Connell as a total villain. After all, he did use some of his seminary students for sexual pleasure, carried on some sexual relationships for many years, and paid off at least three of them to keep them quiet, while he rose to prominence in the Catholic hierarchy. In this light, the students seem to be total victims, groomed for sex under the guise of therapy and deceived thereafter into believing each was chosen for a "special" sexual relationship.

An Irish villain preying on victims in America? Actually, that is too simplistic. From what the students have said, and what the records show, their relationships with O'Connell were much more complex than that. To illustrate that assertion, I'll start with the case of Matthew Cosby, one of the last of the St. Thomas students to be ensnared in O'Connell's web of sex and deceit. As Cosby told it in legal proceedings, O'Connell had been counseling him about his confusion over sexual identity when at one session he suddenly began fondling his genitals until he was erect, while holding him tight in a bear hug. Cosby was scared, shocked and bewildered. The fondling continued in the counseling sessions, in late-night dorm visits and in the priest's bedroom, when they were both naked. Cosby was 15 years old when the sexual encounters began and 23 when they ended, with O'Connell by then a bishop.[15] O'Connell was 25 when he was named to the faculty of St. Thomas, where he was accused of all the sexual activity. He became bishop at age 50, when it continued.

If Cosby was scared, shocked and bewildered at first, why did he allow O'Connell to continue the sexual activity? The answer, according to Cosby, is that he nevertheless considered it to be part of normal behavior and normal treatment in counseling. In fact, it was normal behavior for the young student. He had participated in fondling and even oral sex with classmates before the priest started on him. O'Connell once tried, and failed, to get him to perform oral sex; otherwise it was all fondling, masturbation and touching. Besides, to this small-town teenager, O'Connell was a kind of God who had chosen him to be a priest. And so their relationship went on for eight years. (In my research on O'Connell I found there was homosexual activity among students and priests in three seminaries in Missouri, despite proclaimed efforts by the Vatican to stomp it out. Kenrick, where O'Connell had studied, was one of them.)[16]

Cosby only decided that he had been abused in 1993, two years after he broke away sexually from O'Connell, after talking with a friend who had been abused by an uncle. Writing in a journal for a seminary counselor, Cosby wrote, "Wow, I think I had a breakthrough last night, a real breakthrough. I accepted I was sexually abused and it wasn't my doing, it really wasn't. I cried so much, muffled sobs . . . I lost part of myself, this special boy of 15 I call him. He's so close, he is, but he's so afraid still. I hurt for him because he won't hurt for himself yet. So I cry for him and each tear brings him further out." That is powerful stuff.[17]

But Cosby was not done with the bishop. A few months later he traveled to Knoxville to confront O'Connell, express his anger over how the bishop had hurt him, and to ask why he did it. In the end, it wasn't much of a confrontation. They both cried. O'Connell apologized and said he wanted to show Cosby that two men could lie in bed together naked and touch each other and it didn't have to be sexual. He claimed that wanted to help Cosby realize he was not a homosexual, that this was normal behavior. Cosby didn't buy that explanation, but held back his anger because "at the time I still cared very much for him and wanted him to say he was sorry."[18]

O'Connell was more than sorry; he was worried, worried that Cosby or some of his other sex partners would break their code of silence. Cosby didn't, but Lindsay and Dixon did. The following year, in 1994, Lindsay told Bishop Boland of Kansas City about his sporadic, 23-year sexual relationship with O'Connell. Lindsay says he told him about sex in the seminary, followed by a long-time "friendship," which he would say later included sex in hotel rooms and once, when O'Connell was bishop, at a sleepover in his residence in Knoxville.[19]

Boland kept the information to himself and, astoundingly, suggested that Lindsay deal with his abuser on his own. So Lindsay called O'Connell, who deflected him by saying that he was seeking help and would sin no more. The bishop was safe again, but only for a year.[20]

Dixon was the next to complain about O'Connell, a complaint that ultimately led to the demise of the bishop—and yet another priest from Ireland, Manus Daly. By then a priest himself, Dixon had been assigned to teach at the St. Thomas Aquinas seminary, where O'Connell had abused him years earlier. The problem, then, was that the head of the seminary was Daly, one of two priests who had molested Dixon before O'Connell. And, remember, Dixon had gone to O'Connell for counseling to deal with that abuse and his own conflicted feelings about his homosexual inclinations. Facing Daly again at the seminary, Dixon went into deep depression. Unsatisfied with the response of O'Connell and his bishop to his complaint, he quit the priesthood and threatened to sue the church. The church and Dixon settled secretly, keeping the case quiet for six years.[21]

During that time, however, Cosby and Lindsay began to use O'Connell, the way he had used them for so many years. They began asking for money, for a car, for rent, to furnish an apartment, to deal with financial difficulties. It was not blackmail, but a demand for restitution, their attorney said later. And O'Connell, scrambling to save himself, paid readily and without complaint, writing endearing e-mail messages and sending regular notes. He gave almost $11,000 to Cosby and $21,000 to Lindsay.[22]

"You are in my prayers and affection every day," O'Connell wrote in a note to Lindsay, signing off with "Love, +A." Another time, he said in an e-mail message, "Yes, I realize I have not sent you money in a while—partly because I was trying to build up from helping you with the car before Christmas. But I will SOON. God love and bless you . . . +O'C." Two years later, the bishop was still sending money and he apologized for being late on a bank transfer. Although Lindsay had confronted the bishop over his abuse, he continued to be friendly with him in his communications. He shared his thoughts and concerns, still wishing he could have been a priest, yet expressing doubts about his faith in the church, closing with "prayers and love." The tone of his messages indicates to me that he still genuinely liked the bishop, that he was not just seeking money. The Irish charm had not worn off.[23]

The bishop also was able to maintain a "friendly" hold on Cosby, partly because of the "gifts" but not entirely. As I noted, Cosby said he still cared about O'Connell after the confrontation over his abuse, before the bishop started giving him money. Cosby still "cared" despite an attempted suicide and self-inflicted cutting of himself following the shock of the initial abuse. As he explained later, "I was cutting myself because at the time I was so numb I did not want to feel anything emotionally. I didn't, it was things that were going on with O'Connell, with my life…I shut down emotionally." Although Cosby didn't say so directly, he implied that the other things in his life included his homosexual relationships with other teenagers and confusion over his sexual identity.[24]

O'Connell was supposed to be counseling teenage boys like Cosby to help them feel okay about their sexual feelings, or help a youth like Dixon deal with previous clergy abuse. Instead, he took advantage of them, continued for more than two decades to control them, and caused severe emotional damage, all for his own sexual satisfaction.

Dixon brought him down. When accounts of sex abuse in the American Catholic Church exploded following revelations in Boston, he felt compelled to break the secrecy of his case and go public.

O'Connell wasn't the only priest from Ireland to go down after serving in the small-town Jefferson City diocese of Missouri. Daly returned to Ireland after being removed from a parish. Hugh Behan, also from Ireland, wound up as a greeter at Disney World after he was dismissed from his ministry as editor of the Catholic newspaper—he'd been accused of abusing a girl and a young woman. Behan was fired from his Disney World job when word got out about his past, and was last seen living in a housing tract near Orlando.[25] In better days, Daly, O'Connell, and Father Jim McNally had visited O'Connell's family in Ireland. McNally, of Irish descent, would also be accused of abuse later—he denied it. The large Irish contingent at Jefferson City, which accounted for almost one-third of the priests there at its peak, was badly tarnished. Even the seminary, in which O'Connell had played a key role for so long, was closed down in the wake of the multiple clergy scandals. Why? Partly for lack of candidates for the priesthood. O'Connell, its most successful recruiter, was gone and disgraced.

Was that the end of the story? Not quite. O'Connell, the indefatigable Irishman, didn't give up without a last gasping effort to contain the damage. As I mentioned earlier, he offered more money to Lindsay and pleaded with Cosby not to go public in a lawsuit. Responding to their offers for reconciliation, he begged them for forgiveness and healing. It was much too late; Cosby, Lindsay and others would sue their long-time friend for abuse, and some would express their long-dormant feelings. In a handwritten statement of anguish, Cosby said that "for 19 years I allowed this man to silence me, to force me into a life of depression, anger, sorrow, mistrust, but mostly of numbing, empty silence." Part of his anger, he said in an e-mail message, came from the feeling the bishop "got away with it."[26] Dixon said that O'Connell had betrayed his trust in him, but he felt better knowing he was not alone. "I've exposed him for who he really is," he said. "I wished I had done it sooner."[27]

Michael Wegs was even more critical of the bishop he had once admired. "He should be in jail," he told the *Palm Beach Post*. "He violated the ultimate trust. He corrupted an entire institution. He corrupted the ideals and morals of young boys. But nothing will happen to him. He will not go to jail. He has lost his power and access to Palm Beach society, but he won't suffer more than that. He won't be defrocked. He's just waiting out the storm, and what better place to wait it out but at a southern plantation." He was, of course, referring to the Trappist monastery in a beautiful, secluded area of South Carolina.[28]

Though he was the most outspoken of the bishop's victims, he was arguably the least abused. Wegs, recruited by O'Connell from a largely dysfunctional family, was one of the first students to be sexually involved with him in the late 1960s. In a remarkably balanced portrait of the bishop, Wegs described him as a kindly task master, cheerleader, listener, and Pied Piper leading his students into the priesthood. But then, Wegs said he saw another side of O'Connell during counseling over the bitter divorce of his parents. This was O'Connell asking "creepy" questions of a homosexual nature.[29] During those counseling sessions, Wegs figured the priest was masturbating when he rubbed a stuffed hippo around his groin area. What followed can only be described as weird.

Even though Wegs was turned off by O'Connell's homosexual allusions, he said, he later began performing sexually for the priest late at night in a small room near the altar of the seminary chapel. Again, as he described the scene, he would go to the chapel when he couldn't sleep, light some candles, sip some Communion wine, read a book, and, when he felt the urge, masturbate while O'Connell watched him from the shadows. Wegs said O'Connell appeared to be masturbating himself one time when he moved his hand vigorously under his robe. Six times Wegs performed; six times the priest watched. Why? "I knew that I had done something that pleased him, and that was the goal…I was glad I made him happy because he was my father." That's how Wegs would recall his feelings in a lawsuit accusing O'Connell of abuse in the late-night performances.[30]

I could question whether Wegs' sexual involvement was serious enough to justify his judgment of the bishop later. But that really is not the point. As a journalist, Wegs was able to speak so tellingly for all of O'Connell's victims. And Wegs merely reflected what other former St. Thomas students were saying: their friend, the bishop, was not truly a friend; he had been using them for his benefit. And Wegs continued a campaign against

O'Connell. He and other victims, in a letter to St. Thomas Aquinas seminary alumni, sought the names of more victims, hoping to bring about a criminal investigation.

As I present this dark side of the bishop from Ireland, I am reminded of Fr. Tony Flannery's observation that the priestly sex offenders he knew in his Ireland were also good, kind and caring individuals. That was certainly true of O'Connell. He was a master recruiter of young men for the priesthood. He was loved and admired by the boys in the seminary he ran. As bishop in Knoxville, even while he continued to sexually abuse two young men from that seminary, he campaigned to abolish capital punishment and increase state spending for the poor. He also traveled the world on behalf of Catholic relief programs.[31]

When I told Father Joseph Starmann, who was O'Connell's classmate at the Kenrick seminary in St. Louis, that I was doing research on the life of the bishop, he wrote in an e-mail, "If you ever get to the bottom of the O'Connell story, you will surely have to explain the fact that he could apparently deceive so many people so completely. I can't pretend to know much about pedophilia or pederasty—the whole business nauseates me thoroughly—but one certainly has to wonder how such a rolly-polly, seriously overweight, ridiculously unathletic and physically unprepossessing middle-aged man could manage to seduce so many teenage boys."

I've tried to explain why O'Connell was able to seduce so many boys. As I noted, the Irish factor, the underlying theme of this narrative, played a part. Wegs elaborated on that factor: "His charm and exotic demeanor as an Irishman played to our sensibilities. Look at what he has accomplished. He left his mother country and came to the United States for the sake of God. And he has been successful in his calling, as St. Thomas illustrates."

Of course, O'Connell deceived not only the boys, but also his fellow priests. When I talked to many other American priests who lived with or worked with him over the years, they responded as did family members and priests in Ireland. They were stunned over what he did, had no clues he was doing it, and had nothing but praise for him as a priest and bishop.

Father Patrick Short, who also came from Ireland and lived with O'Connell for nine years, told me, "I was in absolute shock. I didn't go to bed that night. . . . I just couldn't believe it. I know a man makes mistakes, but he had done a tremendous amount of good." Father William Forst, who lived with O'Connell for five years, said he was not aware of any misconduct. "I have nothing but praise for him," he said. Father James Offutt, who has known O'Connell for more than four decades, described him as did the people in Ireland: glib, friendly, outgoing, an Irish ward heeler, a jokester. Nothing at all negative? Well, said Offutt, he told crude jokes—very funny, but very crude.

None of the priests, however, were quite as effusive in their comments on O'Connell as was Hugh Behan, the man removed from his ministry over allegations of sexual misconduct. "Tony O'Connell is a very holy man, a wise and compassionate and loving man," he wrote in one of many e-mail messages. "I never once heard him say an unkind word, never lose his temper, never tell an off-color story, never hint at any sexual innuendo, never use a swear word . . . in the 41 years I have known him." In his testimonial, good enough for sainthood, Behan went on to tell "how pastoral and sensitive and generous and fatherly he was to his priests and people." What about the accusations of nine men? Several of them lied, Behan said.

I suppose I should ask myself: why give credence to the voice of an accused abuser priest from Ireland about an abuser bishop from Ireland? The answer is that I feel all voices should be heard; just as Wegs spoke for victims, so Behan speaks for the accused, especially O'Connell. As I have related, he had plenty to say about the bishop in an exchange of e-mail messages over many months, and in a two-hour interview in his modest home. In addition to his comments on O'Connell, he claimed more generally that priests, in trying to teach sexuality, were caught in "boundary" violations less serious than sexual acts. He also contended that the priests themselves are victims—of biased "Catholic bashing" by the media. He said this is the last acceptable nativist prejudice in America; a prejudice, I should recall, from which early Irish immigrants suffered greatly.

But Behan expressed particular bitterness about the bishops, how they discard clergymen (like him) in what he calls their "unmerciful" policy of one-strike-and-you're-out, which calls for the suspension of a priest on the basis of one credible allegation of abusing a minor. He described it as a death sentence, a violation of human rights, a move by the bishops to save their asses. He also called for democracy in a church now run by bishops. I would add that Bishop Gaydos, one of those all-powerful monarchs, banished Behan while covering up for O'Connell. Now Behan cannot wear priestly garb or celebrate the mass in public. But he retains his Irish pietism, prays, and reads the bible for three hours each morning after midnight, attends mass on Sundays. He also retains the Irish missionary spirit, urging a visitor to return to the practice of the Catholic faith. As for himself, he wouldn't talk on the record about the sex-abuse allegations against him, one of which the church settled by agreeing to pay an undisclosed amount of money to the accuser.

Gaydos would not submit to an interview when the *St. Louis Post-Dispatch* published a comprehensive series of articles on clergy abuses in the St. Thomas Aquinas seminary. Instead he issued a statement admitting the "sordid truth" of what happened there, but decrying a failure by the newspaper to recognize the seminary's accomplishments in training hundreds of young men for ministry. "In the eyes of some," he wrote, "we will never do what is right."

The day before he resigned, more than two years earlier, O'Connell had said much the same as Gaydos when he joined other bishops in calling sexual abuse "both criminal and sinful."[32] Asked later in a deposition about each of the abuse accusations against him, he took the Fifth.

CHAPTER SIX

IRISH SEEDBED

THE IRISH NEWS MEDIA played it up big, and deservedly so, because it was a big story. "Priest Molested 10 Girls on the Altar," was the headline of one report. "Shocking Findings Condemn Church and State," was another, above a picture of accused priest James Grennan with a crooked smile. "Priests Shamed in Damning Report," was still another.[1] The Irish government had come up with the "shocking findings" in an investigation of child sex abuse by Catholic priests in southeastern Ireland.[2] I wasn't particularly shocked, however, because sex abuse among priests and religious brothers has been a growing scandal in this island country, where most of the people are Catholic and sex had long been a taboo subject.

In the 1990s, stories began pouring forth of horrendous abuses that the Christian Brothers and other religious orders inflicted on children in the pervasive system of boarding schools. More recently, the accusations shifted to parish priests—from the small-town Ferns diocese to big-city Dublin. The abuses, whether in the schools or the parishes, are not new; they have been a long-standing curse in the church, with boys and girls the victims. What is new is that the government and the church have investigated, uncovered, and admitted the crimes, and the Irish media have finally broken the shackles of cultural censorship to let the people know the truth about "The Lie of the Land."[3, 4]

As I noted earlier, I had gone to Ireland to examine the causes and extent of the abuse problem in that country, hoping thereby to determine why so many priests exported to the United States wound up as sexual predators. One of the most prominent of the predators was Bishop Anthony O'Connell, whose sexual involvements I examined in the two preceding chapters. Next, I will look at the big picture and consider some of the key questions, such as: just how extensive is the abuse by priests in Ireland? More than in the United States? Is there something in the culture of Ireland and the church that caused so much abuse among the Irish clergy, in both countries?

In my quest for answers I sought an interview with Bishop William Walsh, partly because he presides over the western Ireland diocese that produced Bishop O'Connell, and partly because he is a prominent liberal who I hoped would offer an honest take on the sex-abuse crisis. This is the bishop, mind you, who has defied the pope to favor the ordination of women to the priesthood.

Walsh is not impressed by rank and status—his own or that of others. He turned the long driveway of his mansion into a public parking lot, and later converted that mansion into church offices. Personally, he prefers to be called "Willie."

Walsh agreed to meet with me in a sparsely furnished room. He came in alone; no secretaries, attendants or other acolytes for him.[5] I expected him, as an outspoken liberal, to be of the flamboyant type. He was not. Dressed in dark trousers and a dark blue sweater, topped with an unruly shock of white hair, he spoke slowly, carefully and seriously. "Should I call you Willie?" I asked, hoping to establish a friendly rapport. "You can call me anything you want," he answered without smiling. Trying a bit of flattery, I told him that Tony Flannery had called him "the best we have." No, Walsh said, he prefers not to be singled out. He's just one of the members of the college of bishops.

Pleasantries aside, I got to my point: How well did he know Bishop O'Connell and did he have any thoughts on that abuse case? Walsh said that he'd met O'Connell a couple of times, but he wouldn't comment on individuals. Was there much public reaction in Ireland to the O'Connell case? No, he said, O'Connell was not well known.

But this unusual and controversial bishop did comment on the abuse scandal wracking his intertwined church and nation. "Be careful about saying sexual abuse is present across society," Walsh said, "because if you suggest that, one is in some way excusing what happened in the church as an institution and certainly I would not be one to say that. It is a very significant scandal. It has been a serious breach of trust. It has caused enormous pain to victims and families, and I would not be one to minimize that." Some defenders of the church have contended that abuse is greater in Irish society generally than in the clergy. Walsh said there are no studies to prove that one way or the other. But he pointed to "some evidence" that the incidence of abuse appears to be higher in Anglo-Saxon countries such as Ireland, the United States and Canada, than it is elsewhere.

Well, how much abuse has been inflicted on Ireland? Having read so much about the assaults on children in that country, I carried the bias that it was far worse than in America. My judgment was premature, and might be wrong (or right). Much of Ireland's bad reputation comes from the terrible treatment of children in boarding schools, which have been closed since the 1980s. The American church never ran such a system, although Canada did and is now paying the price for similar mistreatment. No one, including Bishop Walsh, knows whether sexual abuse among priests in the parishes and day schools of Ireland has been any worse than in the United States. No one knows because there are no comprehensive Irish studies that would answer the question. The American bishops sponsored a definitive investigation of abuses among their priests, but Ireland is just beginning to look into this matter.

What the Irish government has uncovered so far is bad enough, however. It also mirrors my findings on the unusually high level of abuse of girls. The three-year government inquiry into the southeastern Ferns diocese found that 40 percent of the abuser priests had molested girls, like the ones at the altar during confessions. This is somewhat less than my estimated level of female abuse in America among priests from Ireland, but it is much higher than the ratio for all the Catholic clergy abusers in the United States.[6] And the details of the abuses in Ireland are just as terrible as in America. As the victims told it, the notorious Father Grennan, now deceased, would hear their "sins" while committing his own, putting their hands to his genital area. This priest, scruffy of dress and smelling of alcohol, allegedly tried to sexually penetrate one girl at age seven. She committed suicide at age 31. Three other girls tried to kill themselves as a result of the abuses of other priests.[7]

If Grennan was bad, Martin Clancy was worse. The report of the government inquiry said this priest molested children, including the rape of "very young girls," over a period of almost 30 years, using his position as manager of a local public school to gain access to his victims, one as young as nine. The report described how he allegedly abused five girls, made one pregnant and raped another on a weekly basis until she was 12. Judy, also age 12, told the inquiry about going into his house for sex-education classes: "I was a child when I went to that room in that house but when I left I was not a child."[8] She had gone there, as directed by the principal of her school, to learn about sex. Clancy, who has since died, removed her underclothing and fondled her, intimately and painfully. Like other errant priests, he took the childhood out of a child. Unfortunately for the children, there was no separation of state and church in Ireland, so they were at risk even in the public schools.

In pursuit of their perverted sexual satisfaction, these "celibate" priests fondled, penetrated, impregnated, and raped girls in such various venues as automobiles, residences, and churches. One caressed a girl's breast while she practiced music. In the United States, a priestly preference for boys has been partly attributed to the fact that the priests have more access to boys. But the Irish priests in both countries have not lacked access to girls. In all, the government inquiry identified 25 priests who allegedly abused more than 100 children in the Ferns diocese. (Many of the priests, though not all, denied the allegations.) Although the abuse of girls was unusually high in Ferns, the rate was higher for boys. The most infamous abuser in that diocese was Father Sean Fortune, who committed suicide at the start of his criminal trial for molesting eight young men. He died of a drug overdose, at age 45, dressed in his priestly garb and holding a rosary, a prayer book nearby. In the later Ferns probe, he was accused of abusing 26 boys.[9] Remember that in this country with an oversupply of priests, the parish clergymen were the chosen ones, the elite, while many of the others, considered to be second-class, of lesser distinction, were exported to the United States.

Elite or not, these men often became sexually involved before they were ordained to the priesthood. St. Peter's College seminary, which educated Fortune and other students for the Ferns priesthood, was a virtual breeding ground of abuse, arising from what the inquiry found to be a high level of sexual activity among both students and faculty. One former seminarian called it "an academy of debauchery." Many of the priests from St. Peter's— ten within one short five-year period—later were accused of abusing children. That was almost half of the abusers identified in the inquiry. One of the worst faculty offenders was Fr. Donal Collins, teacher and then principal, who consistently molested boys for 20 years before he was finally called to account and sent to prison for gross indecency and assault. In a bizarre manifestation of his perversion, Collins would visit a dormitory at night to measure the penises of the boys under the pretext of ascertaining whether they were growing normally. With abusers like Collins on the faculty, it's not exactly surprising that there would be molesters like Fortune among the students, or that the authorities would have failed for so long to derail their careers. Actually, according to the inquiry, the church ordained Fortune as a priest despite clear signs he had abused boys at the seminary.[10]

St. Peter's was not the only seminary to face problems over sex. In a sensational report a few years ago, an Irish newspaper cited complaints of homosexual relationships, sexual harassment, and sexual abuse at St. Patrick's College in Maynooth, the premier seminary in the Irish church. Following up on these allegations, the Ferns inquiry found that a faculty member, Monsignor Michael Ledwith, had been named president in the mid-1980s even though some seminarians had labeled him a homosexual who initiated sexual "friendships" with certain students. Sure enough, two decades later the monsignor was accused of having molested a teenage boy for two years prior to his promotion. Ledwith, who had held prominent positions in the Vatican, resigned and went to the United States.[11]

I am reminded of young men telling me of sexual activity in American seminaries. In both Ireland and in the United States, despite efforts to "form" the students to live a celibate or sexless life, sex was hardly an alien concept for the adolescent boys or their adult educators in these all-male institutions. These Catholic boys had been taught to avoid sex and reject impure thoughts; shouldn't they have been able to slay the devil of temptation? Not necessarily. As the sexist cliche goes, boys will be boys, regardless of religious belief. I recall that in my public high school some of the adolescent boys talked incessantly about their sexual relationships with girls. In the seminaries, lacking girls, some of the Catholic boys form "particular friendships" with other boys, or, yes, with their teachers. Anthony O'Connell was one of those abusing teachers in an American seminary. Donal Collins was another in an Irish seminary.

When the friendships or relationships become abusive, however, the authorities, whether bishops or high-school principals, are supposed to stop it. Often they do not, in Ireland as well as the United States. Consider how Bishop Brendan Comiskey dealt with—or failed to deal with—four of the most egregious cases in the Ferns diocese, involving Fathers Collins, Grennan, Fortune, and Clancy. The Ferns inquiry told an amazing story of Comiskey's malfeasance: he lied to law-enforcement officers and the news media; he failed to report abuses to proper authorities; he allowed priests to continue in the ministry despite credible allegations of child abuse; he believed the denials of his priests without bothering to talk to complaining children. By failing to deal properly with the complaints of these children, the inquiry said, he prolonged their suffering. When Collins was assigned to another diocese, for example, Comiskey didn't bother to tell the bishop there that the children were at risk from the priest. Mind you, these were priests who were abusing boys and girls for years and years, while Comiskey and other church authorities responded feebly, if at all.

The inquiry was direct, but not harsh, in its criticism of Comiskey, using words like "regrettable," "flawed decision," "seriously mistaken," and "incorrect." What it all came down to, according to the inquiry, was that Comiskey did not seriously consider the welfare of the children while protecting his priests. Why was that? In my earlier investigation of the sexual involvements of Catholic bishops, I found that some prelates accused of sexual misconduct had been easy on their errant priests, possibly fearing exposure themselves if they were too tough. O'Connell, a multiple abuser, was accused of that. On his part, Comiskey was reported to have taken solo vacation trips to Thailand, where he stayed at a hotel used by prostitutes, including young males. Comiskey told the Ferns inquiry that these "rumors" were "false and evil."[12] He resigned over allegations that he had protected pedophile priest Sean Fortune.

I have no way of knowing whether Comiskey was compromised by personal impropriety. As I have noted, however, he was timid in dealing with allegedly abusive priests. As bishop he recommended Monsignor Ledwith to head St. Peter's seminary, telling the Ferns inquiry later that negative information about Ledwith "had simply gone out of his head." He didn't believe the girls who said that Father Grennan had sexually molested them at the altar. And he took two years to "persuade" abuser Fortune to see a psychiatrist, leaving him unmonitored in his parish during that time.

The bishops in Ireland and the United States had plenty of other motives for the way they covered up and condoned the sexual misconduct of the priests and other bishops. I've mentioned how they were trying to avoid scandal in the church, but they also sought to save the careers of colleagues and maintain a tradition of church secrecy. Comiskey manifested another powerful influence: a desire to protect his own kind, that is, his priests. In the Grennan case, he gave "unquestioning support" to the priest, according to the inquiry, and saw no need even to talk to the alleged victims. He felt the girls just weren't credible, even though he knew that a government agency involved in the case felt they were.[13] As for Fortune, Comiskey assigned him to a new parish despite the abuse complaints against him, noting that his "very priesthood was at stake." Whether he liked it or not, the bishop said, "He is one of our own." (Doctors and police officers, of course, also protect their own.)

The Ferns inquiry, with great attention to detail, sheds a lot of light on why the church response to sex abuse has been so lacking. Comiskey is the prototype. He was slow and indecisive in dealing with abuse claims, didn't follow up on the complaints, deferred to medical and legal advice rather than rely on his own judgments. When he did get such advice, it was sometimes ill-founded because he hadn't ensured that it was based on all the appropriate information. Add faulty memory. He didn't remember that one priest had admitted abusing a child. And lack of knowledge. At one point, he used the oft-repeated rationale that he didn't know much about sex abuse, though he had been dealing with such cases for seven years. Some of this can be attributed to shoddy management and poor record-keeping. If all that were not enough, Comiskey also had a drinking problem. Is it any wonder that this bishop, and undoubtedly many others, allowed sex abuse to flourish in their church?

Comiskey typifies a general failure of leadership that has been well documented and reported in Ireland and the United States, the two countries most noted for priestly abuse of children. Remember Cardinal Mahony of Los Angeles. Much of what was said of Comiskey also was said of Mahony in his dealing with priest pedophile Oliver O'Grady. He lied. He forgot. He covered up. He took no responsibility. The difference is that Comiskey resigned when the Fortune case blew up. Indeed, the Ferns inquiry commended him for recognizing his failure to deal properly with that priest. Mahony, on the other hand, denied everything, went on to become a cardinal and lives on, enjoying power and prestige in Los Angeles.

Aside from individual differences between church authorities, the scope of the scandal was quite similar in the two countries. After the Ferns report was released in 2005, the church reported the following year that it found in the large Dublin diocese that 102 priests were suspected of having abused at least 350 children. That report doesn't have the credibility of the government's Ferns inquiry because it came from the church. But the government is filling the credibility gap with an investigation of Dublin, and may follow with a national inquiry. Even then, I'm not faulting the church probe. It was comprehensive and included a key component missing in Ferns: the percentage of priests accused of abuse. More than 3.6 percent of the Dublin priests were alleged abusers in the 65 years of that study, somewhat less than the 4 percent abuse rate for American priests in the 52 years examined in that national study. The longer time period in the Dublin study, however, covering years when abuse was seldom reported, could mean that the abuse rate was considerably higher than in the states.[14] In fact, the Ferns inquiry found that only a handful of abuse cases were reported to that diocese before 1990. The children were too intimidated to tell their parents, or the parents were too trusting of the priests to believe them.

In giving credit to the Dublin report, I should mention the response of Colm O'Gorman, a victim of Fr. Fortune's abuse, who then became a leading advocate in Ireland for other abuse survivors. In a time when church authorities are often criticized for their response to the sex scandal, he praised Dublin Archbishop Diarmuid Martin for being open and transparent about the problem in his diocese. Before Martin took over in Dublin, he said, "the leadership was suggesting they didn't really understand the nature of the problem. We're not hearing that kind of nonsense any more."[15] Nobody's credentials on this issue are better than O'Gorman's. He runs an advocacy and support organization, One-in-Four, based on research indicating that one-fourth of Irish children have suffered sexual abuse. It was his organization, in fact, that pushed the government into undertaking the ground-breaking Ferns inquiry.

Naturally I wanted to talk to O'Gorman about the subject of my inquiry when I was in Ireland. He treated me first to a short lecture on Irish church-state relationships. "The church has been more politically powerful than the state," he said. "We lived in a theocracy. The state and society depended on the Catholic Church in education, health and social services. And I've had government ministers acknowledge that legislation, especially sexual, was overseen by the church."[16]

I asked him about the horrible abuses in the Irish boarding schools, which were funded by the government but run by religious orders. "When you create an institution given unquestioned and uncontrolled dominion over children, you attract people who abuse, because they have a target group, with no parents or guardians. It's a sweet shop for them."

They were far worse than sweet shops. They were houses of horror, these so-called industrial schools, these detention homes for abandoned or neglected children, the children of unwed mothers, children who got in trouble, children of families too large for the parents to provide for them. Journalist Mary Raftery described their plight in three television documentaries, *States of Fear*, that shook up the nation and led to a long-running state investigation. She followed up with a book, *Suffer the Little Children*. As Raftery and co-author Eoin O'Sullivan reported, tens of thousands of children, many viewed as illegitimate or unworthy, were physically and sexually abused for many decades until the schools were mercifully closed.[17]

Again I offer a bit of history from the book *Fallen Order*, as context for what was happening in Ireland. While working on this narrative, I read how priests of the Piarist order, founded in Rome in 1600, preached sexual repression (as the Irish would later), while they were abusing children (as the Irish did later in Ireland, America, and Canada). The Piarist schools were originally intended to provide a free education for poor children, but they evolved into private academies and spread across Europe, teaching the children of prominent people, the likes of Mozart, Goya, Schubert, and Victor Hugo, along with kings, emperors, and a future pope. Little did these members of the elite class know that a sexual abuser once had become head of the order, or that the founder, bishops, cardinals, and even the pope were covering up a scandal. The pope ultimately shut down the order, but it was revived and exists today.[18]

The Irish boarding schools, however, never catered to the elite. Throughout their time, they ill-served the poor and hapless. The worst of the worst was the Artane industrial school, which, like most of the others, was run by the Christian Brothers. According to Raftery, Irish police took more than 300 statements from former residents at the schools, alleging sexual and physical abuse against up to 100 Christian Brothers.[19] She said it was one of the biggest police investigations of child abuse ever, anywhere.

While staying in Ennis in western Ireland, I went to a Christian Brothers school there to talk to Sean McNamara, a religious brother in the order, who had taught at Artane in the 1950s, when Ireland was still an extremely poor country. How bad was it at Artane? McNamara started by telling me how bad it was all over Ireland at that time. Life in the 1950s, he said, was extremely hard—no indoor water, toilets, or heating. You could say the children were better off in the institutions than in their own homes. Because he was not involved in the dormitories, he said, he didn't know of anything happening there and was never accused or questioned about anything. He had 40 to 50 boys in his classes; they took up all his time. He left after three years and was glad to be gone. The school was run in the military style because of the number of students; you had to be a sergeant major. If you were soft you were seen as silly, and he was regarded as silly or soft. If you expressed a contrary opinion, you were told to shut up. And you would think twice about going to the people in authority. Did he believe the allegations of abuse? They are probably true, he answered. The staff members were too young to handle their responsibilities.[20]

This gentle, thoughtful man gave only a grudging admission of abuses by the religious order he cherished, at the school where he worked. He said he was not aware of those abuses, just as the priests in the United States who lived with Anthony O'Connell said they did not know that he was preying on young men. (And the Christian Brothers have claimed that sexual abuses at Artane were far less than reported.)

Looking back on my visit with Sean McNamara, I feel a certain sadness about him and his order of beleaguered brothers and priests. He was one of two aging religious brothers I met at the Christian Brothers school in Ennis, where O'Connell had received his secondary education. I felt the same about Father Frank O'Neill, the Jesuit, meeting me in the seemingly empty quarters of once-vibrant Mungret College, where O'Connell was educated in philosophy. In some ways, they are symbolic of the decline of the Catholic Church in Catholic Ireland. The church that for many years ran the country has given way to the materialism of growing prosperity and the public disgrace of escalating scandal. Two years after I met with Frank O'Neill, his Sacred Heart Church in Limerick was closed and sold, to be converted into a pub according to one news report.

When I stopped to see Fr. Patrick Conway, pastor of Christ the King Church, O'Connell's home parish, I got the same sense of malaise. He's a missionary priest with the Columban order, just returned from 17 years in South Korea. Devastated by reports of the scandal, he told me of a meeting of Columban priests to discuss how they felt about it, and whether they could come up with reasons why it happened. They couldn't. They felt betrayed by their fellow clergy, about the "terrible evil" they had perpetrated on children. "We were going through an awful time," he said, "and didn't know how to cope. Many felt hurt and ashamed." Part of their anger, he said, was directed at the bishops, including Comiskey, for allowing the abuse to go on. As for the priests, he wondered how they could abuse boys and then go out and distribute the Holy Sacrament—the body of Christ—at communion. He and other priests felt self-conscious themselves about appearing at mass in front of the congregation. Conway poured out his soul in a tiny office of the church. What could I say?[21]

Tony Flannery also had plenty to say about the devastating effects of the scandal in his native Ireland. "For one church in a small town, attendance is down 50 percent," he said. "Sexual abuse is a factor in that. It had a major effect on the attitude of young people. At the time, the church was in decline anyway. Young people were rebelling. Parents and the church were doing their best to hold the line. Then this thing happened."

Tony Fahey, a research professor at the Economic and Social Research Institute in Dublin, was so kind as to send me a chapter from a book he and colleagues were writing on changes in religious values and attitudes in Ireland.[22] They generally support the views of Flannery. Fahey and his colleagues noted that Ireland had been on the "upper edge" internationally in regular church attendance and the importance people attached to God in their daily lives. The unprecedented internal shocks of the sex scandals in the 1990s, along with other factors, helped change that. Catholic Ireland began to slide into retreat and decline, they wrote. The church could offer no defense for a series of sordid revelations. Weekly church attendance fell by 25 percent in just over a decade. The sharpest drop was found among urban young adults. Less than a quarter of Catholics have a great deal of confidence in the church. Fahey and his co-authors concluded that the Irish had shifted from a strong attachment to the institutional church to a lukewarm orientation towards formal religion. This loose attachment, rather than outright rejection, could become the defining feature of religiosity in Ireland. In other words, Ireland is becoming more like Catholic America—more secular and less religious.

Declining church attendance is only the half of it. The nation and the church face the prospects of paying more than $1 billion to compensate the victims of the abuses, a staggering sum for such a small country.[23] And the church is suffering ever more shame as continuing investigations, and reports of more abuses, add to the scope of the scandal. Three bishops have resigned and a major voice in the once-compliant press called for all of them to resign, subject to papal reappointment of the good ones, to help restore their credibility and moral authority.[24] Beyond that, an exodus of priests and a lack of candidates for the priesthood have led to talk of importing replacements, this in a land once known for a surplus of priests.

So this is what the Irish Catholic Church has come to—a church in crisis, as one author described it.[25] This is the church that has been given credit for helping to save European civilization during the dark ages, when Irish monks and scribes preserved the West's written treasures, and Irish missionaries brought back the Christian religion to a land overrun by barbarians.[26] These are a people who, many centuries later, survived a devastating famine, many by fleeing to North America in "coffin ships."[27] And this is the church that educated and exported thousands of priests to serve the religious needs of the millions of Irish immigrants in America, only to help cripple the same church through the mistreatment of children.

For the people of this small nation, it is a huge tragedy worthy of their theater, a tragedy of their own making.

CHAPTER SEVEN

CELIBACY AND SEX

I T WAS A DARK, RAINY DAY in western Ireland as my spouse and I
waited on the highway for a bus to return to our hostel in Ennis. We had
just visited the famous Knock Shrine where in 1879 as many as 20 people,
young and old, claimed that the Virgin Mary had appeared before them,
bathed in a brilliant light, looking to heaven as if in prayer. Many of those
people were desperately poor, having survived a terrible famine, and looked
to their religion for comfort. Now, more than a century later, in a prosperous
country, pilgrims still walked silently around the shrine, rosary beads in
hand, seeking succor from the woman they call the Holy Mother of God.
And down below at the bus stop, a middle-aged Irish woman, drenched in
the rain, told us that she had filled containers with holy water from the
shrine, which she and a friend would drink for good health. Unusual? Not
Ireland. On an earlier visit, we had seen people lined up waiting to fill plastic
bottles from a spring where Mary had appeared before three children; at
least that's what the children said, and the people believed them.

Beliefs and believers, churches and the churched, priests and piety—
they make up the widely shared image of this land today, even though the
religious fervor of the people has receded and the power of their priests has
diminished. For all their lingering religiosity, as shown at Knock, many of
them have been severely shaken in their faith upon learning of a sickness in

93

the body of their church, the sickness of widespread sexual abuse of children, the sickness represented by the seminary principal, by the priest at the altar, or by the prominent clergyman inappropriately named Fortune.

I was determined, upon going to Ireland, to get the answer to the one overriding question: Why? Why has there been so much abuse among the priests? Is the answer to be found in the peculiar Irish culture, or is it to be found in the Catholic Church itself? The answer may be in both. In years past, a cultural celibacy repressed or restrained the natural expression of sexuality, while a church-imposed celibacy sought to prevent all sexual activity, natural and unnatural, in the priesthood. Both attempts to impose celibacy backfired, as demonstrated by the unusually high rate of sexual abuse in Irish society at large, and the alarming amount of abuse by Irish priests.

I can't prove that imposed celibacy caused the abuse, but the association of the two in Ireland poses the possibility that it does. In presenting this possibility, moreover, I am not attacking celibacy in the church as such, because it can be a noble sexual denial that enables priests to devote their lives to religious service, as my priest brother Jim has done. I am, however, providing evidence that suggests it might be a factor in the abuse scandal, and deserves greater study and consideration.

The Ferns investigators, in their inquiry into priestly abuse in southeastern Ireland, declined to propose any single cause of the problem. Their conclusion is worth quoting in full:

> Overall, the literature searches and consultations carried out by and on behalf of the inquiry would lead it away from associating child sexual abuse solely with issues such as sexual orientation, celibacy, sexual dysfunction, relationship problems, traumatic childhood experiences, previous victimization, loneliness, isolation, problem drinking, immaturity or other social or psychological factors. Any of the above features could be associated with most of the incidents reported; however, focusing on single causes fails to acknowledge that many people, including priests, who experience these factors in their lives, do not abuse children. [1]

I would agree that there is no conclusive evidence of "single causes," but I wish that the Ferns investigators had looked more closely into the underlying factors that might help explain Ireland's clergy abuse problem. One possible factor is the alarming rate of sexual abuse in the society at large, apparently higher than in other countries, which may have carried over into the priesthood. As I noted earlier, a pioneering national survey of more than 3,000 adults determined that one in four men had experienced sexual abuse as a child.[2] Comparing those results with studies in the United States and Europe, David Finkelhor, a leading American expert on the incidence of sex abuse, reported that the Irish rate is higher than both the European rate and the relatively high North American rate. "Note particularly the extremely elevated level, in comparative terms, of childhood victimization reported by Irish men," he wrote. "It is three and a half times higher than even the level reported by North American men."[3] (Irish women reported a childhood abuse rate of 30 percent, which is higher than for men, but not much higher statistically than the 20 to 25 percent rate for women in North America, Finkelhor noted.)

Tony Flannery, the Irish priest I have quoted so often, was one of the childhood victims. In his book *From the Inside*, he tells of twice being abused as a boy and young man. First, a workman "gently" molested him when he was seven or eight years old, paying him half a crown for it each time. Later, when he was a young student at a junior seminary, the school president—Flannery believes he was gay—"emotionally abused" him at a private meeting, by sitting closely beside him, putting his arm around his shoulder, and asking Flannery whether he had any bad thoughts or urges, or had "done anything" with himself. The encounter left him feeling guilty and exposed, though he acknowledges that the president might have meant well.

For years after, Flannery says, he felt continued guilt and shame, as though he had done something bad to deserve the long-ago abuse. Still, he survived and moved on to become a priest in the Redemptorist congregation of itinerant preachers, who go from parish to parish to help people renew their faith. When I met him at an Irish pub, Flannery—now in his 50s—seemed balanced and at peace with himself.

But many men never overcome the trauma of childhood abuse. In fact, as a leading international expert on sex abuse pointed out in a study organized by the Vatican, one-third of pedophiles were themselves victims of sexual abuse.[4] Oliver O'Grady, whose story I told earlier, was one of them. Given the rate of abuse in the culture at large, then, it is hardly surprising that Ireland has had a serious problem of sex abuse among its priests.

There is more in the Irish survey to support this reasoning. That survey also found that women reported an even higher rate of childhood abuse than did men—close to one in three. That shocking rate correlates with my finding that priests from Ireland have been more likely to abuse girls than have been American Catholic clergy. I would say that the Irish priests seem to reflect their Irish culture.

I suggest that the high rate of Irish sex abuse may also be related to a second underlying factor: the overwhelmingly Catholic culture of Ireland—almost 90 percent of the population. That's the view of Mary Raftery, the journalist who produced the stunning revelations of an epidemic of abuse in Irish Catholic institutions.[5] I asked her whether the Irish culture helped account for the prevalence of abuse. That's only speculation, she said, because there are no studies. But she added her own speculation, that it has more to do with Catholicism and the Catholic culture. Indeed, I would say, the Irish culture is the Catholic culture, although that is changing dramatically.

"You would expect that the culture, the repression of sexual activity, would manifest itself in all kinds of unhealthy ways," Raftery continued. The critical question of "why" in the Catholic Church, she said, is answered in part by the attitude of those in authority who covered up and tolerated the abuse. "Ireland exported that kind of attitude toward children, attached less value to children," she said. "The ranks closed as soon as some one was discovered." I would agree that this Irish Catholic culture was a strong factor in the repression and cover-up, the silence and secrecy, and the concern for the image of the church more than for the welfare of the children, that allowed the sexual abuse to flourish. As Raftery pointed out, and as I have found to be the case, it was this culture that was exported to America.

In making her case for Catholicism as a root cause of the sexual abuse in Ireland, Raftery referred me to the book *Eunuchs for the Kingdom of Heaven* by German theologian Uta Ranke-Heinemann. Ranke-Heinemann argues that the church through the centuries denigrated sex, degraded women and "championed a perverse ideal of celibacy." She writes about "a Christianity that once moved about in daylight turned into a discreetly darkened whisper in the confessional, which increasingly and ever more indiscreetly concentrated on the sins of the flesh."[6] She could have been writing about me in my youth, when in confession I felt compelled to embellish my sins of lust to measure up to the expectations of the priest.

I also found support for Raftery's viewpoint from Tony Flannery. When I asked him about the root of the problem, he said, "It's both culture and church. For so long, they were identical. They worked hand in hand. One thing you can say for sure, the church caused sexual repression. If a child is abused . . . it is because the priest is a pedophile or because he has been repressed." Flannery does not, of course, contend that all sexually-repressed priests are abusers. As he sees it, some sublimate their sexuality through prayer and sacrifice, others find an outlet in hard work, and still others, in alcoholism. As for pedophiles, he says, some chose the priesthood as a safe place for access to children.[7] (Serial pedophile O'Grady said he chose the priesthood because he thought he would enjoy the work, but he used the opportunity to fulfill his warped sexual desires.[8])

I was glad that Tony mentioned alcoholism, because it could be another underlying cause of endemic Irish priestly abuse. We all know the stereotype of Irish drinking, but this one, like many other stereotypes, has some truth behind it. While the men of Ireland drink less than some other Europeans, such as the French, many still drink far too much. According to government surveys, a quarter of the Irishmen consume more than the recommended weekly limit of alcohol, often in binge drunkenness.[9] So what does that have to do with sex abuse? In a Vatican study, Professor Ron Langevin of Canada's University of Toronto asserts that alcohol abuse appears to be "far more important than mere coincidence," especially as it relates to violence toward victims.[10]

The case of Fr. Michael Simpson, a serial abuser from Ireland, is a powerful example of what Langevin is saying. As I noted in Chapter Two, Simpson allegedly inflicted sexual violence on at least eight girls in Washington state, including the rape of a 10-year-old. All the while he was drinking heavily, so heavily that his bishop, Nicolas Walsh of Yakima, apparently unaware of his sexual activity, sent him back to Ireland to be with his family. Then Walsh sought an Irish bishop who would accept him for part-time priestly practice, with Walsh generously offering to pay part of his salary. Before dumping him on Ireland, Walsh and his predecessor, Bishop Cornelius Power, had tried and tried to stop Simpson's drinking, which had almost killed him at one point. They were sympathetic to one of their own, Power having come from Ireland and Walsh being of Irish heritage. Their efforts, through treatment and exhortation, were spelled out in correspondence from the 1970s obtained by attorney Kosnoff for a lawsuit.[11] In one letter, an exasperated Power wrote that he had been told for three years of Simpson's excessive drinking, sometimes while functioning as a priest. Later he told Simpson he knew he wanted to "come home" from treatment, but urged him to continue, recalling how, as a lonely boy at age 14, he, the future bishop, wanted to leave the seminary but his mother wouldn't allow it.

The bishops were sympathetic? "Father Simpson is a very good priest," Power said in still another letter. "He has had great difficulty admitting and facing his problem." Almost three years later, after Simpson returned to Ireland, Walsh expressed his interest in Simpson's health and welfare, concluding that his priest would function better in Ireland than "in a missionary diocese where there are so few protections." Walsh also said that three of his priest advisors, including two from Ireland who knew Simpson well, had recommended he write to Simpson and urge him to stay in Ireland. As for the Irish connection, Walsh wrote later of being proud to be a coworker and friend of the priests from Ireland, "because of their dedication to and love for the church but also because of my own Irish heritage." Dedicated or not, Simpson never conquered his problem of alcoholism, nor did he overcome his sexual addiction for girls.

This personal correspondence of the bishops and Simpson provide a rare look into the close and accepting relationship among Irish priests in America, not always to the benefit of the people of the church. I would argue that this troubled priest should have been removed from the ministry early on, when it became apparent he was denying his addiction and would do little or nothing to cure it. More importantly, the Simpson case shows how heavy drinking can prompt men, especially those from the repressive culture of Ireland, to express their sexual desires in bizarre and criminal ways.

I should point out that Ireland is hardly the only country to suffer the consequences of a culture of sexual repression. When I was in Saudi Arabia on a news assignment, I saw an example of a much stricter enforcement of sexual morality and a rigid separation of the sexes, and I read how men gathered in the desert, sat in circles, and masturbated. Similarly, in describing a stifling political and sexual repression in China in earlier years, a journalist told how male students in art classes stampeded to see pictures of nude women, and expressed desperate urges in bathroom graffiti, "Forgive my forthrightness. I want sexual intercourse."[12]

Or, consider the results of the sexual repression of Islamic fundamentalism in Iran, a theocracy that makes the Ireland of the past appear almost liberal. In the "repressive gender apartheid" of that Middle Eastern country, ruled by male clerics and an autocratic ayatollah, there are reports of police taking young women to provide sex for the wealthy and powerful mullahs, of women being sold into sex slavery, of girls at home suffering from domestic abuse and parental drug addictions. The Tehran police chief, who enforced a strict dress code for women, reportedly resigned recently after being found naked in the company of six nude prostitutes in a local brothel. In whatever country, sex is often the aphrodisiac of power, but it also can be the downfall of powerful men.

Of course, not everyone agrees with Raftery that Ireland has been rife with sex abuse because it is so Catholic. Donal Leader, a prominent member of the Christian Brothers, which has been accused of most of the abuse in the boarding schools, said church people feel that Raftery and those who follow her line are trying to demonstrate that the influence of the Catholic Church has been almost always negative, and an obstacle to a more tolerant and liberal Ireland. He doesn't buy that; he feels the problem has been exaggerated, especially by the tabloid media. But Leader finds some truth in the argument that if sexuality is repressed it is bound to find some form of expression, sometimes deviant and criminal.[13]

I can't draw a hard conclusion that repression is to blame for the Irish scandal. After all, the American clergy, in a more open sexual climate, also have perpetrated a large amount of sexual abuse. When I asked Bishop Walsh for his explanation, he responded, "Both extremes [repression and license] lead to abuse. There is always the challenge to get the right balance in our lives. Sexuality is such a strong force in all of us. Either extreme is going to lead to some destructive forms of abuse of sexuality."

When I asked Hugh Behan (the Irish priest accused of abuse whom I quoted in Chapter Five) about Irish repression versus American freedom, he was quick to chastise me: "Your seeming naivety about the U.S. sexual culture versus the Irish and your seeming assumption that the U.S. culture of 2004 was the same as in the 1950-60 decades astounded me."[14] A valuable point. I remember how the church in those earlier years, heavily influenced by Irish Catholic priests, tried hard to suppress sex in movies, books and all other aspects of our lives. I seriously doubt, however, that the repression was as widespread and effective as in Ireland. Behan, by the way, wouldn't talk on the record about the abuse allegations against him, but he told me that he has "repented of any deviation of the path."

Wherever it tried, in fact, the church couldn't stamp out sex even during the puritanical 1950s and early '60s. Irish author John Cornwell gives a remarkably candid account of being an English seminary student in those days. In *Seminary Boy*, he tells how even as he and other young men were being groomed to lead sexless lives, they were obsessing about sex and engaging in sexual activity of many kinds. Or at least Cornwell was. He fell deeply in love with a fellow student who kissed him, masturbated night after night, indulged in the "mortal sin" of sexual fantasies, then became obsessed with women and enjoyed French kissing. A priest and another student, meantime, tried to molest him. Before entering the seminary, Cornwell said, he had been sexually abused by a stranger and had joined in molesting a girl. "With vicious associates I assaulted a girl in a disused bomb shelter, holding her down while we put our grubby hands down her knickers," he recalled. Cornwell left the seminary after five years, quit the church, got married, and later rejoined the church.[15]

Cornwell, whose mother is native-born Irish, was obviously confused about his sexual orientation when he entered the seminary at the age of 13. In Ireland, many of the boys who went into seminaries in years past also were quite young, making me wonder whether this could be another reason for the high abuse rate among Irish priests in Ireland and America. The younger the boys upon starting clergy studies, the more sexually immature they would be upon entering the priesthood. Another sex-abuse expert in the Vatican study noted that some newly-ordained priests, because of emotional immaturity, experience stress in developing adult relationships. As a result, they seek comfort in relationships with adolescents. The risk? "A significant number of incidents of clergy sex abuse of teenage boys takes place in those first years after ordination," said Dr. William Marshall of Queen's University in Canada, who is a director and consultant in sex-offender programs.[16] He was one of the experts participating in the Vatican symposium on sex abuse, which I cited earlier.

Many Irish priests probably were prone to be abusers partly because they were immature sexually, not just from being so young going into seminaries, but also as a result of the sexually repressive Irish culture. In fact, the Ferns report said that "immaturity" was among factors that could be associated with the clergy sex abuse uncovered in that inquiry. Consider that the abuse-prone Irish Christian Brothers for years recruited young boys in their schools by asking them to sign a form stating they wanted to join the order. A lot of the boys, as young as 13, signed the statement innocently, recalled Seamus O'Reilly, a student in the early 1970s at the Christian Brothers school in Ennis and now editor of the *Clare County Express*. Sexually immature? "They were just waking up physically," said O'Reilly.[17] Brother McNamara told me that the practice, which has since been dropped, was like Army recruiting and did lead most students to join up, around age 14. "If they were older," he said, "they might change their mind."[18] These sexually naïve boys, many seeking an escape from the poverty of early Ireland, became Christian Brothers priests, prone to be abusers.

Barry Coldrey, a Christian Brother in Australia and the leading authority on sex abuse in his congregation, estimates that 10 percent of the 4,000 members of the international order abused young people, more than double the reported rate for other priests in Ireland and America. "The sexual abuse of minors—and general clerical infidelity to celibacy vows—has been the dark underside of the old Irish-Australian working class church, covered over many years by tribal loyalties," Coldrey writes.[19]

Of course, the Christian Brothers were not the only sexually immature young men from Ireland who became abusers. Fr. John Lenihan told one of his victims, Mary Grant, "What happened was that I developed a strong feeling of . . . of affection for you because, I guess I was going through maybe the same kind of growth thing that had never taken place in my life up to that point. I had come through a system of, you know, Irish farm background. All-boys high school. All-boys seminary. I never had a date in my life. I had never gone out with a girl. I had never had a dance." Lenihan made up for lost time in California. He engaged in oral sex with Grant, who was 14 at the time, and admitted to her he had gotten another girl, 16, pregnant, taking her in for an abortion. There were others as well. Eventually he agreed to leave the priesthood.[20]

Anthony O'Connell was not so young when he entered a seminary in the States, but he had shown no interest in girls while a young man, according to a boyhood friend. Was he emotionally immature? And thus, as an adult, did he seek comfort in relationships with adolescents? And did that lead him to start sexually abusing them in the first years after ordination? My research on O'Connell's early life indicates that the answer is "yes" to all of the above. To support that answer, I turn to Michael Wegs for a description of O'Connell, known as O'C, when he was a teacher at St. Thomas Aquinas seminary in the States. "Unlike the other faculty members who remained aloof," wrote Wegs, "O'C was the one we could tease and joke with, the person who would play with us, and the one adult who could act our age and understand our mindset. His essential charm and magnetism was that we could identify with him and he with us."[21] As I wrote earlier, Wegs was one of the students to claim that O'Connell sexually abused him in his early years after ordination.

If sexual repression, a fact of early life for O'Connell and many other Irish priests, can lead to sexual abuse, the obvious question is whether celibacy, the lifelong suppression of sexuality for all priests, compounds the propensity for abuse among clergy. One expert in the Vatican report wondered whether imposed celibacy was a risk factor for abuse, a concern apparently not shared by Vatican officials.[22] The Ferns report said an expert group "was unanimous in its view that the vow of celibacy contributed to the problem of child sexual abuse in the church."[23] Professor Eamonn Conway of Mary Immaculate College in Limerick gives a more tentative opinion: "It has to be conceded that mandatory celibacy may make the priesthood attractive, perhaps even unconsciously, to people with psychosexual problems," he writes in a paper dealing with cultural issues in the abuse crisis. "Together with a naïve understanding of the power of prayer to overcome human weakness, many men may have seen, and still see, the commitment to a celibate vocation as a way of escaping having to deal with sexual immaturity."[24] In line with my speculation, I would add that because they failed to deal with their sexual immaturity, many Irish priests became abusers under the cover of holy celibacy.

Today, it may seem odd to write of sexual repression in Ireland, given how sexual mores have changed. Just consider the sex offerings I noticed on newstands during my trip: "Hello Boys! How My Breasts Feed My Self-esteem," read one headline in the *Sunday Independent*, showing a woman's barely covered front.[25] "Will She Go the Distance?" asked the *Sunday Times*, as the pictured woman licked the tip of a cigar and tugged on her panties.[26] Or, consider the large study of teenagers in the Galway area found that one-fifth of them were sexually active, the median age being 15.[27] Another recent survey concluded that "young Irish people are gambling with unprotected intercourse—and getting caught."[28] The government itself reports that one in three births is now outside of marriage.[29] I could go on.

Mary Kenny, in her article, "The Last Fanfare of Good Old Catholic Ireland," says the mildly saucy songs of the early 1950s, decried by clergy, were the leading edge of a wedge "which now makes full sexual intercourse available on late-night TV and anything in the sensuous line that you choose accessible via the internet."[30]

How are the people taking this? Consider how they reacted when a Catholic priest in rural Ireland (the last bastion for conservatism?) admitted to fathering a child with a local school teacher. According to the news story, they refused to get worked up about it, closing ranks in his defense. "People are understanding," said a pub owner. "It's 2006. Everybody twists the rules a bit on their way through life." Even a 73-year-old priest.[31]

In some ways, Ireland has come almost full circle from its sexually permissive early centuries, before the Catholic Church imposed rigid controls over sexual behavior. Extramarital sex, multiple partners, and homosexual relations were more or less the order of the day in these pagan times. Four centuries after the birth of Christ, the former shepherd-slave Patrick, a Romanized Briton, came along to help convert the island to Catholicism and change the warrior mores of the tribes. But, says historian Thomas Cahill, Patrick's influence had little effect on the sexual mores of the pagan culture.[32] The kings reserved the right to deflower every bride before yielding her to her husband.[33] Even the Irish monasteries were not especially devoted to the rule of chastity.

Over a thousand years later, Ireland was definitely a Catholic country, but under English rule the church was in no position to impose its rules of behavior. In the 1700s, the English imposed penal laws that forbade the practice of the Catholic faith. At that time, Catholic Churches were destroyed and priests were forbidden to live in the country; many were executed.[34] Not until the latter part of the century did the British release their grip, allowing what author Fintan O'Toole describes as a deep but relaxed spirituality in which the broad culture's mores continued to prevail over devotional and behavioral rules.[35]

The horrible famine of the mid-1800s changed everything. A fungus destroyed almost all of the life-sustaining potato crop, killing more than one million people by starvation and disease, and causing a mass exodus of almost two million to North America. According to one historical account, the poor peasants believed themselves partly responsible for the famine crisis, making them more attentive to the priests who preached against recklessness and advocated sexual restraint, chastity and delayed gratification.[36] In effect, says another historian, the priests took control of the Irish people's sexual lives, hammering away at the horrors of sex outside of marriage, advising single men and women to avoid physical and social contact.[37] Accordingly, men married later, even practiced a non-priestly celibacy, sometimes sublimating their sexual desires in alcohol.[38]

In the wake of the great famine, celibacy was imposed not just on priests, but was practiced by a stunning one-third of Irish men in the general population. Did this culture of celibacy help foster the child-abuse problem that has persisted into the twenty-first century? And did alcoholism exacerbate that problem? I can only speculate, though there is some foundation for this possibility. The 2003 church-supported study of clergy sex abuse noted that child abuse was an issue in Ireland even going back to late 1800s.[39] Further, clergy abuse expert Richard Sipe documents that the culture in Ireland at that time sustained a pattern of child abuse.[40] As I have noted, celibacy can involve a repression of sexuality, which might cause emotional immaturity, often cited as a factor in child sex abuse.

The Catholic Church was not solely responsible for Irish sexual repression in those years. As historians point out, the priests were responding to the economic and social pressures of the times.[41] After the famine, many people lacked the land and money to marry early and raise children, and they needed the church to help sustain them spiritually and emotionally through those years of celibacy. The priests also were reflecting a rigid morality derived from Victorian Britain and a negative view of sex as propounded in the conservative seminaries in France, where they trained during the British suppression of Catholicism.[42] I return to German theologian Ranke-Heinemann for her reference to the so-called Jansenist influence in France and the English-speaking Catholic world, an influence that decried the evil of sexual pleasure.[43]

For more than a century after the famine, these priests and their bishops ruled the tiny nation of Ireland, ran its public schools and social-welfare programs, dictated to the government, and regulated the moral behavior of its citizens. In so doing, they helped create an Irish culture that, in the words of historian Jay Dolan, was "moralistic, scrupulous, legalistic, very much hung up on sex. It was heavy into penance, ridden with guilt, focusing on sexual improprieties."[44]

Ranke-Heinemann documents the sexual obsessions of church authorities throughout history, their bungling efforts to decide whether pleasure could be allowed in sexual intercourse, or their attention to the details of whether the woman should be allowed atop the man in the act of sex for fear his seed might spill out of her vagina. This obsession over sex was a worldwide concern of the Catholic Church, but it had a profound influence in Ireland simply because Ireland was so Catholic. Ireland, in turn, became a seedbed of sexual deviance among many of the "male celibates," the clerics who became predatory priests.

The sex scandals of the priests, which hit the public like a cluster bomb in the 1990s and thereafter, was a devastating blow to a church that was already in decline. Author Louise Fuller, in her book *Irish Catholicism Since 1950: The Undoing of a Culture*, describes how rising prosperity and the modernizing Vatican Council II already had begun to liberalize Irish society, weakening the power and influence of the once-triumphant Catholic Church. The scandals sped up the decline, according to opinion polls, undermining the moral authority of the church and curtailing the devotion of its followers.[45] Journalist Fintan O'Toole concludes that the church is mortally wounded.[46] Priestly critic Brendan Hoban writes of "Irish Catholicism in Crisis," doomed to a continuing decay if it fails to reform itself.[47]

I do not wish to suggest that all, or even most of the people of Ireland are deserting the church and giving up their faith. When I visited Anthony O'Connell's childhood parish in Ballynacally, the pews were full during Sunday mass. But the faithful have been battered by wave after wave of scandal. In that small country church, the *Curate's Diary* implored, "Our Lady of Knock, pray for us." Pray, indeed.

CHAPTER EIGHT

THE POPE
AND IRELAND

Pope John Paul II loved Ireland, and the people of Ireland adored him. He showed his love by visiting the nation in 1979, just a year after becoming pope. "Young people of Ireland, I love you," he said at a youth mass. And the people showed their love for him by turning out in huge numbers—one-third of the population, the Irish press estimated—to see and hear him.

It was not surprising that Karol Wojtyla had a special affection for the tiny country. It was (and is) one of the most Catholic nations in Europe, a Europe that had become more and more secular and less and less Christian. And it represented a conservative Catholicism of rigid church doctrine and strict personal morality, a religiosity that Wojtyla, as Pope John Paul II, would espouse for the next quarter of a century.

At that time, John Paul suggested that Ireland was at the crossroads, one road leading to a prosperous and confident future rooted in its Christian past, the other heading to a "soul-less future, rooted in rampant consumerism and the glorification of the individual over the community."[1] Family values, he said, would be tested in this new Ireland. Standing at the pope's side were Eamonn Casey, one of Ireland's most prominent bishops, and Fr. Michael Cleary, the nation's most famous priest.

Maybe the pope didn't know that the Irish church had already embarked down the wrong path, a path far worse than one of individualism

109

and soul-less consumerism. Even as John Paul spoke, a religious brother in a Catholic school raped a boy who had not been allowed to attend the pope's mass in Limerick as punishment for absconding.[2] It was awful, but hardly unusual. For decades, church people had been sexually abusing children at the Catholic boarding schools of Ireland, a scandal that would not be publicly exposed for many years to come.

What's more, the pope probably didn't know that the "men of God" by his side, Bishop Casey and Fr. Cleary, had already fallen off the path, engaged in torrid sexual relationships with women. If only the Holy Father had known that these "defenders of the faith" had blatantly defied the family values of which he spoke.

If only he had known that Bishop Casey, the loyal preacher of sexual morality, was sleeping with Irish-American Annie Murphy, making love in the bishop's palace, his holiday home, a New York hotel, and even in a car parked in a gravel pit. If only he had known that his bishop sired a son and then cast off both mother and child for years, supporting them secretly with church money to buy their silence.

Or if only he had known that Fr. Cleary, a radio and television personality described by Fintan O'Toole as a passionate defender of conservative values, had fathered two children with his housekeeper, Phyllis Hamilton, an incest victim who, homeless at age 17, had gone to him for help.[3] He certainly didn't know that Murphy and Hamilton would tell their stories more than a dozen years later, Hamilton describing "My Secret Life as a Priest's Wife for Twenty-Seven Years." The pope's Ireland, the bedrock of his church, was already crumbling—not because of the external pressures of materialism the pope preached against, but because of corruption and hypocrisy within.

In my opinion, the Casey and Cleary stories reveal that the pope was living under an illusion, an illusion that his chosen clerics were as sexually pure as his beloved Virgin Mary, the woman in white who supposedly had appeared to all those people at Knock. As part of his visit to Ireland, John Paul had gone to Knock, endorsing that purported Marian apparition (and many others) as a historical fact. These extraordinary claims are not universally accepted, even by Irish Catholics. I was told that some parish priests were upset about these "appearances" of Mary—often before children—because they prompted the faithful to divert money from their parishes and give to the Marian enterprises. But John Paul had a childlike faith in Mary. He claimed that, as "Our Lady of Fatima" in Portugal, she had saved his life in an assassination attempt.[4]

The Irish people also loved Mary, the desexualized mother figure, as sociologist Tom Inglis describes her. "The model of modesty, virtue and humility, which priests and religious provided, was maintained in the home through a growing devotion to Our Lady," Inglis writes. "Our Lady may have been popular in Ireland before the nineteenth century, but it was then, as part of the devotional revolution, that the rosary, novena, May and October devotions, as well as shrines, processions and pilgrimages made in her honor, become common practices. These practices reached their peak in 1879 in Knock, County Mayo."[5] It was an appropriate place for the pope to warn of rampant consumerism and glorification of the individual. (The new pope Benedict XVI, in meeting with Irish bishops, also called on Our Lady of Knock to "watch over and protect" the Irish people.)

The Irish Catholic Church had staged this "devotional revolution" after the great famine of the mid-1800s, creating a theocracy that persisted for generations, until it was weakened from within by corruption, abuse, and hypocrisy in the sanctuaries of clerical power. I've described how the sex scandals, along with secularism and consumerism, brought about the decline of this empire in Ireland.

Fr. Raphael Gallagher, a moral theologian, told me that Ireland is now heading toward the Italian model. "People may go to church three or four times a year, or for a wedding or funeral," he said. "They have not abandoned the church, but they have established a new rhythm of practice."[6] Irishman Gallagher is well-positioned to compare Ireland and Italy; at the time I interviewed him, he had been in Rome for six years, serving on the faculty of the Alfonsiana Academy. It is well-known that the Italian people have a relaxed view of Catholicism, far removed from the past devotional fervor of the Irish.

Travelling to Rome, I sought to learn whether the problems within the Irish church mirrored a culture of sexual hypocrisy within the Vatican itself. After all, the Irish Church in its glory days was a reflection of the strict morality promulgated by the Vatican. Did imposed celibacy and sexual repression lead to illicit sexual expression in the Vatican as well as in Ireland? I spent two months in Rome searching for an answer to that key question.

What I found should be no surprise: the male celibates in Rome cannot always enforce sexual purity in their own ranks, let alone in the provinces of Ireland and America. Yes, some of these men of Rome, even a cardinal "prince" of the church, have been involved in the forbidden sexual activities themselves. Beyond that, in the case of the cardinal and others, the Vatican set the example of denial, secrecy, and cover-up, an example the American and Irish bishops followed, exacerbating the sexual abuses in their countries.

In fact, Pope John Paul II himself set the example in his reaction to the compelling evidence that Cardinal Hans Hermann Groer of Austria, one of his favored conservatives, was a sexual predator. He ignored the claims of abuse and refused to call for an investigation, remained silent on the suffering of the victims, then effusively praised the cardinal after he died. This case is worth close attention because it says so much about the mentality of the Catholic Church's highest authorities when faced with sexual problems.

In 1986, John Paul appointed Groer, a Benedictine priest, as an archbishop; two years later, he was promoted to cardinal. Not only was Groer a conservative, he also shared John Paul's devotion to the Virgin Mary. The Virgin was evidently not the model, however, for Groer's personal morality. In 1995 came the shattering revelations: after the cardinal had publicly denounced priestly abusers of boys, five former pupils at a seminary high school were prompted to accuse him of molesting them when he was a priest. One of them, Josef Hartmann, said Groer "tempestuously" embraced him, French kissed him, sat on his lap, rubbed his penis and stroked him all over, sometimes when he was talking on the phone. "I have seen myself as . . . his whore," Hartmann said in an interview. He was 14 years old at the time.[7]

What makes this case so relevant to my inquiry is how the pope responded when he learned of the abuses. In fact, he didn't respond at all for five months; then, he defended Groer against "violent attacks" and thanked him for his "generous and faithful" service to the church. When Groer finally stepped down as archbishop of Vienna, the pope said it was because of his age—he was 75. The pontiff did not mention the allegations of abuse as a factor in the resignation.[8]

But that was only the beginning of the story. A priest, himself claiming he had been sexually harassed by Groer, would disclose in an interview that 10 years earlier he had warned authorities at Gottweig Benedictine seminary, including Abbot Clemens Lashofer, about Groer's "homosexual tendencies."[9] The response was typical: church authorities went easy on Groer and kept the dispute in the family. Abbot Lashofer tried to get Groer and his accuser to "heal the wounds and to solve the conflict by talking to each other." Lashofer did not investigate whether Groer had been abusing anyone else.

The Vatican was even more derelict in dealing with Groer. When he was up for appointment as archbishop, the Vatican delegate in Austria didn't ask about Groer's background, contrary to the usual consultations about candidates. Groer was on the fast track, given special treatment then and thereafter. Even after Groer resigned as archbishop, Abbot Lashofer named him prior, second in command at the Gottweig monastery.[10]

Groer stayed on that job for three years, until new allegations of abuse arose, prompting massive protests in Austria. Only then did the Vatican, at the request of Abbot Lashofer, ask the Benedictines to investigate their Benedictine cardinal, again keeping it in the family. And only then did the pope ask Groer to relinquish all duties in the church, no longer appear in public as a bishop, and leave Austria. Even then, Groer later violated the agreement, presiding at a baptism, appearing in public in his red robes.

When Groer died at age 83, John Paul praised him "for his great love for Christ and his church."[11] Why did the pope defend him to the end? I asked that question of Marco Politi, a veteran Vatican journalist. He said a Vatican source told him that the pope initially thought Groer was under attack because he was too conservative, and later defended him out of pity for an old man. That's loyalty to the grave.[12]

While the sexual accusations against Groer ignited a major public controversy, most of the sexual activity in the super-secret nation state of the Vatican remains hidden. Only a few insiders, for example, knew that an Italian bishop had died of complications from AIDS. He spent his final months in the VIP suite at the famous Gemelli Clinic in Rome, where prelates and popes are treated. The Vatican took precautions to keep it a secret: the bishop was known at the clinic only by a number, and access to his room was possible only by a private code. After his death, no autopsy was performed. The cause of death given on his death certificate was congestive heart failure. Because he was not a homosexual, speculation at the clinic was that he contracted AIDS from a prostitute.[13] (In a similar case in America, Bishop Emerson Moore of New York died of AIDS at a remote hospice in the state of Minnesota; his death certificate listed him as a laborer in manufacturing.[14])

Officially, of course, there is no sex in the Vatican, headquarters of the pope, cardinals, bishops, and priests who run the Roman Catholic Church. All sexual activity is forbidden for these consecrated celibates. But during my two-month visit in Rome, I found that rumors of sex among the prelates— mostly between men and women—were widely circulated among Vatican journalists and insiders, even if almost never investigated. There is no tradition of objective, investigative reporting in Italy. An anonymous group of Vatican prelates, however, blew the dome off St. Peter's Basilica in their book *Via col vento in Vaticano*, an exposé of sex and corruption worthy of the tabloids. The book portrays a daughter blackmailing her father the bishop, scandalous relationships between priests and nuns, and quick transfers to cover up sexual affairs or abuse.[15] Translated as *Gone with the Wind in the*

Vatican or *Shroud of Secrecy* in English versions, the book enjoyed runaway sales after the Vatican tried to suppress it by prosecuting Msgr. Luigi Marinelli, the only author to identify himself. *The New York Times* covered the story under the headline, "Tell-All Book Creates Furor at Vatican."[16]

Marinelli, a veteran Vatican bureaucrat now deceased, and the other authors named no names and mistated some of their "facts." However, information from Vatican insiders and other credible sources indicates that at least three clerics do indeed appear to fit the circumstances cited in Marinelli's book.

One is a Vatican bureaucrat who allegedly was apprehended by police, half-naked with another man in a parked car—an incident, with no names given, published in the Italian press. ("I don't recognize myself in the descriptions," the priest told a Dutch newspaper.)[17]

Another is an archbishop who, after only three years heading an archdiocese in Italy, was transferred to a Vatican job following an accusation that he sexually abused a young man. (In a letter to me, the archbishop said of the alleged sexual abuse, "It is a question of only suspicions that are pure calumny." In another letter, he said he asked for the transfer because "I was not able to overcome the difficulties I encountered in governing this beloved diocese.")[18]

A third is a prominent Vatican diplomat, now a cardinal, who was shipped from Jerusalem to Argentina when it was learned that a story would be published about his alleged "cordial relationship" with a nun. (The cardinal told me by telephone from Italy that he didn't respond to gossip, but when I asked again about the allegation, he denied it and said, "Maybe it was a confusion with one of my secretaries.")

Hans Groer is not the only bishop close to the pope to be publicly accused of sexual improprieties. Archbishop Juliusz Paetz of Poland resigned following allegations he sexually molested young seminarians and priests. Paetz, who had organized John Paul II's extensive early travels and worked for more than a decade in the Vatican, denied the allegations. "Not everyone understood my genuine openness and spontaneity toward people," he said.[19] But another priest told an American journalist, "He was always on the make."[20] The Vatican was slow to investigate him, as one of its own. As I have reported throughout this book, young boys enter Catholic seminaries at their own sexual risk, whether in America, Ireland, England or Poland.

Stories about the alleged sexual interests of Bishop John Magee of Ireland, secretary to three popes (including John Paul II), have also circulated for years. Ireland journalist Sam Smyth told me that he investigated, and found no support for, an allegation that a "rent boy" had been sent to the Kensington, England, hotel room of Magee one time more than a decade earlier. On the other hand, an inquiry for Ireland attorney Simon Kennedy found anecdotal evidence that a call for a male prostitute allegedly had been made from Magee's room, but the call boy and a man were refused entry to the hotel. A spokesman for the bishop, in a long letter signed off "with every good wish," told me that an investigation more than 10 years earlier concluded that the allegations were unfounded; he called them a "malicious lie." (The spokesman did not respond when asked for details of that investigation.)[21] Even then, the rumors rose up again recently in the Vatican. Who gave birth to the rumors? It was the British government, said Smyth, citing a "credible source." The Brits were out to get Magee, he said, because of his role seeking to help settle the Irish hunger strikes against them in the 1980s.[22]

Another priest close to the Pope, Marcial Maciel Degollado, founder of the Legionaries of Christ, was accused of abusing more than 20 young seminarians and young priests in his religious order many years ago. Maciel called the allegations "defamations and falsities," and John Paul protected him throughout his time as pope. After all, Maciel also was a conservative and his religious order churned out many conservative priests. When I went to see the large estate of the Legionaries in Rome, surrounded by high walls, a picture of a snarling dog on the gate warned me to keep out. (In a surprise action, the new pope Benedict XVI finally forced Maciel to give up his public ministry, at age 86. He died less than two years later.)[23]

Inside the Vatican, where sex may be repressed but talk of sex is not, other allegations also persist. The late Bishop Alois Wagner, a Vatican representative at the United Nations, lived with his housekeeper, who was known as "Mrs. Wagner," according to a former Vatican insider. And another former insider, who is gay, said that Cardinal William Wakefield Baum was known as "Lady Wakefield." Some priests in Washington, D.C., in fact, claimed that Baum was an active homosexual in Washington before his transfer to a top job in the Vatican. Baum, now retired and ailing at age 76, insisted in a telephone interview that he was neither homosexually active nor inclined, having lived "chastely throughout my entire life."[24] Whatever may be the truth behind the allegations about Baum, the Vatican is known as a dumping ground for prelates who get in trouble, such as Cardinal Bernard Law, who was forced to resign for covering up massive priestly abuse in Boston. Law wound up with a sinecure at a prominent basilica in Rome.

It would not be a crime for Baum and other clerics to be homosexual; but tolerating actively homosexual priests is hypocritical for a church that declares such activity intrinsically disordered and gravely sinful. Indeed, in the Vatican enclave of celibate men, I learned that homosexual activity is commonplace—from Swiss Guards at the bottom to prelates at the top. According to credible gay sources, liaisons are arranged in St. Peter's Square, parks, and gay bathhouses. Homosexual Vatican bureaucrats hit on each other. One private survey found a high incidence of HIV virus among seminarians. In a research project, cited by Vatican journalist John L. Allen Jr., a German sociologist was propositioned 64 times by priests in the environs of the Vatican. Moreover, clerics are said to regularly recruit male prostitutes known as "rent boys" near Rome's busy railway station. Among those allegedly seen seeking companionship there was a Vatican diplomat, an archbishop recalled to Rome years ago because of his sexual behavior abroad. When papal attendant Enrico Sini Luzi, a well-known figure in males-only bars, was murdered in Rome in the 1990s, police said marks on his body were consistent with sadomasochistic foreplay.

117

More recently, a popular Italian television priest, Pierino Gelmini, was accused of sexually abusing nine former residents of his "encounter centers" for young alcoholics and drug addicts. Denying the allegations, Gelmini said his accusers tried to extort money from him and went to police when he refused to pay, according to journalist Allen. Going on the offensive, he blamed a "Jewish-radical chic" for a defamation campaign against the church, a claim he later apologizing for making. I was reminded of the famous Irish television priest Michael Cleary, accused of fathering two children with his housekeeper. As I have noted, the Cleary case helped lead to the unraveling of the church in Ireland; will the Gelmini allegations further undermine the church in Italy? (Gelmini has since quit the priesthood, so he could defend himself, he said, without involving the church.)

And if Gelmini weren't enough, another sexual scandal, this one involving a Vatican official, was reported in November 2007, just three months after the Gelmini story broke. Msgr. Tommaso Stenico of the Congregation of the Clergy was caught on a hidden video camera declaring himself gay and making sexual advances to a younger man. According to the *New York Times*, Stenico, age 60, was suspended after the video was shown on Italian television. The cardinal denied he was gay, called the filming a trap, and said he was only pretending to be gay to gather information about "those who damage the image of the church with homosexual activity." Cardinal Julian Herranz, head of the Vatican disciplinary committee, didn't accept that explanation, saying such cases cause sadness, even though they are "exceptions."

In my search for sexual activity in the Vatican, I went from the nondescript apartment dwelling of a prominent gay activist who had threatened to expose homosexuality in the church hierarchy, to the hillside home of a women's religious congregation that exposed sex-abuse among clergy in Third World. I also tracked down a gay former member of the Swiss Guard who had told of homosexuality in that elite corps. The former guard, Franz Steiner, had said in a magazine interview, "When I entered the Vatican, the command advised us that guards who were discovered to be homosexual would be immediately sent back to Switzerland. Thus I had to conceal it, but it wasn't difficult. When I left the Guard, I learned that other colleagues were also homosexual. I understand that one can be gay in the heart of the church, at all levels. It is enough to keep quiet." Yes, in the heart of the church.[25] Steiner, whom I found working in a flower shop, declined to say any more to me.

As part of my quest in Italy, I also talked to former Vatican bureaucrats, church reformers, university professors, members of religious congregations and many journalists who seek facts among the endless rumors in this secret world. I can say it was one of the most frustrating and fascinating experiences in my 40 years of journalism. Frustrating because I was not able to penetrate the Vatican walls to talk with actual church officials, with one exception. In fact, I couldn't even get press credentials from a nun who acted as a Vatican gatekeeper; she didn't trust my motives.

Most fascinating was my interview with Vladimir Luxuria, the stage name for Vladimiro Guadagno, a transgender performer who runs a disco and challenges the homosexual hypocrisy of the Vatican. (Recently, he was elected to the Italian parliament.) Luxuria told me about priests who take "rent boys" to their flats for sex, a priest found on the street dressed as a woman, and a well-known monsignor who is a homosexual. How did he know the man is a homosexual? Gays have a sixth sense about it, he said. Luxuria also talked about his efforts to organize a "World Gay Pride Day" to coincide with the church's Jubilee Year in 2000. As part of that, he announced plans to expose gays in the Vatican but backed off, he said, after receiving an anonymous letter asking whether he would be dressed as a man or a woman in his tomb. "There is a lot of hypocrisy," he said. "A lot of, you can do it if you don't say it. A lot of people say, do it and say it. We don't want to feel guilty any more. We were burned by the church in the Middle Ages. The Vatican has said it was wrong to do what it did in the Crusades, but it doesn't say 'mea culpa' about what it has done to gays."[26] What the Vatican would do, I might add, was blame homosexual priests for the sex-abuse crisis.

I had walked a long way from a bus stop through a working-class neighborhood to find Luxuria's apartment, tastefully furnished, opening to a lovely patio. I enjoyed the visit with a gracious host. Later I walked up the hill to the home of the Missionaries of Our Lady of Africa, to talk with Sister Marie McDonald. I was honored to learn that I was the first journalist she had agreed to meet since the public revelation a year earlier of her report on how priests and bishops were sexually abusing, even raping, religious sisters, mainly in Africa. Unfortunately, she would talk to me only off the record, in view of the sensitive nature of her findings. I had to accept that request considering her report had been criticized for challenging the church publicly rather than keeping it in the family, and for being an example of white people judging black people in Africa. Since my focus was on sex in the Vatican, I had gone to talk to her about credible reports that some impoverished religious women from Third World countries, studying in Rome, had felt compelled to trade sex for help in their studies—to the extent that religious congregations had set up a safe house for their protection. I enjoyed that visit, too, even if Sister McDonald declined to talk publicly about how male celibates in Rome were crossing the line for sex with women.[27]

Women like McDonald have been among the most outspoken and courageous reformers challenging the male leadership of the Catholic Church. I spent a lot of time in Rome at sessions of a "shadow synod" featuring many of these women, along with like-minded men, seeking access to the priesthood for women, married men, and homosexuals. In 2001, they requested a dialogue with the hierarchy to present their concerns at a meeting of the all-male Synod of Bishops. Unsurprisingly, the bishops ignored them. Women have been victims of bishops and priests throughout the world, but not participants in their rule of the church. Meanwhile, buried in the Vatican newspaper at that time was a notice that the pope had accepted the resignation of Bishop Joseph Hart of Cheyenne, Wyoming. No mention was made of the fact Hart had been accused earlier of sexually abusing two teenage boys. The male celibates not only ignored the appeals of the women, they also were spared a reminder of the sexual problems in their all-male world.[28]

Continuing my inquiry, I visited with Reginald Foster, a maverick Vatican bureaucrat who talks from time to time with journalists, making him a rarity in papal circles. (Foster wrote the acceptance speech for Joseph Ratzinger, days before he became pope.) When I asked about the possibilities of sexual activity in the Vatican, Foster said such matters were of no interest to him. I could understand that; for 35 years he has labored in a small office translating Vatican documents into Latin, quite removed from the controversies embroiling the church he loves. But then he volunteered a couple of rather lewd jokes and recalled allegations of homosexual activity involving a Vatican bureaucrat, as well as Bishop Patrick Ziemann of California, and even a past pope. Yes, Foster is a man, and most men pay some attention to sexual matters.[29]

If Foster is symptomatic in professing to be unaware of any sex problems in the Vatican, one would expect Vatican officials to be equally unknowing of such problems, or more likely, not to speak publicly about what they know. They could hardly admit to any breach in the wall of sexual morality they seek to erect around the church worldwide. But they could certainly blame the burgeoning abuse scandal in the United States on the loose morality in that country. And that is what they did, back in 1993. They condemned America, as though Rome were sexually pure.

My friend John Thavis, writing for the Catholic News Service in Rome, quoted a Vatican spokesman as suggesting then that the cause of the abuse scandal in America could be attributed to "a society irresponsibly permissive, hyperinflated with sexuality, and capable of creating circumstances that can induce into grave moral acts even people who have received for years a solid moral formation and education in virtue."[30] He was referring to priests, of course. The same year, the pope concurred that a lack of family values and morality among the American people contributed to the problem. Then, a few weeks later, as if to make sure the blame was properly placed, the Vatican released a statement saying that clergy sex abuse was only an American and Canadian problem,[31] as though those two countries had been more permissive, for a longer time, than the European countries. Not quite.

To correct the record, many American priests were sexually abusing children decades before the American culture became "hyperinflated with sexuality." America was still largely a prudish society up through the 1960s, and the Catholic Church did as much as it could to keep it that way. I know, because I was part of the church's effort to promote sexual morality and "decency." (I later dropped out of that crusade.)

No mention was made in the Vatican statements of any sexual problems in Ireland, a mirror of Vatican morality presumably immune to the permissive, sexually-inflated influences from across the Atlantic. But surely the Vatican would have known, if the Irish bishops were giving honest reports in their regular meetings with the pope, that there was a sex-abuse problem in the Irish church. Surely the bishops knew of the long-standing abuses in the Catholic boarding schools, abuses by the notorious Father Sean Fortune, and abuse by less prominent priests.[32] Also by that time, Bishop Eamon Casey had been caught up in the scandal.[33] Irish society was well on its way to becoming a sexually permissive nation. But the Vatican chose not to admit that the sex-abuse problem had infected other nations, where it had not yet been widely publicized in the news media.

Not until June 1999, after sexual abuse in Ireland had exploded into a major public scandal, did the pope have anything to say about the problem. Even then, he didn't make a major pronouncement on the matter, as he had on the North American scandal. In an address to the Irish bishops in Rome, buried deep in his remarks he referred to the "terrible scandal" of some priests, and professed to be close in prayer to their victims. John Paul II didn't talk about the corruption within the church, but again blamed the "pressures of the surrounding culture."[34] Of course, priests and religious brothers had been sexually abusing boys in the Catholic boarding schools for many decades, while a strict morality still prevailed in Irish society. (Six years later, the pope said nothing about the devastating Ferns report on sex abuse in southeastern Ireland.)

As reports of the abuses surfaced in other countries, John Paul eventually dropped the "permissive society" explanation. But the pope did not give up his longstanding defense of celibacy, despite questions about whether this ban on marriage and sex contributed to the sexual involvements of the priests. "These scandals," he said in an address, "and a sociological rather than theological concept of the church, sometimes lead to calls for a change in the discipline of celibacy." But God's will and the living tradition of the church, John Paul asserted, clearly affirm "the consonance of celibacy" with the sacramental character of the priesthood. The celibacy rule would not change. (Interestingly, it took the Western church 11 centuries to declare that it was God's unchanging will for priests to be single and celibate; meanwhile, the Eastern Church has always allowed married priests.)

Much as he might have wished it, the late pope could not expect universal agreement among his priests about his pronouncements on celibacy, even in strongly Catholic Ireland. Fr. Tony Flannery, for instance, has expressed his opinion that "there is a probable connection between compulsory celibacy, the traditional Catholic attitude to sex and the human body, and the incidences of sex abuse by clergy and religious."[35] Bishop Willie Walsh doesn't speak to possible cause and effect, he just calls for an end to mandatory celibacy, allowing priests to marry if the loneliness and isolation are too much to bear. At the very least, he says, the question should be open to discussion—a debate the popes have so far rejected.[36]

As shown by Bishop Casey and priest Cleary, celibacy is already being ignored by some clergy in Ireland. Peter De Rosa, former dean of theology at Corpus Christi College in London, now living in Ireland, writes that the Vatican is well aware that in some dioceses—and even entire countries— priestly concubinage is practiced as widely today as it was during the Middle Ages and the Renaissance.[37] This assertion is widely accepted among experts on the priesthood. It is this reality, critics argue, that has compromised the Vatican and prompted the pope to close off debate lest this truth be exposed. According to one critic, if the Roman authorities allowed some priests to be married, "priests all over the world would want to marry their mistresses."[38] Would honest marriage be more scandalous than secret concubinage?

Although John Paul II defended the status quo in his address to the Irish bishops, he conceded that changes in Irish society made the "proclamation of the gospel" more difficult for priests. The exaggerated individualism that sometimes accompanies increased material prosperity, he said, has brought a declining sense of God's presence and the meaning of life, as well as a rejection of morality. Knowledge of the faith, along with religious practice, is declining, he added, admitting there is a belief that the church no longer has anything relevant to say to the people of today. What are the bishops to do to turn the tide? Maintain the integral part of Irish Catholic life and ensure that the true content of Catholic doctrine is taught effectively, while supporting new groups and movements to meet changing needs.

The pope's speech, however, was too lacking in specifics to translate into a call for reform. Here is John Paul's advice to the bishops:

> The specific mission of lay men and women is the evangelization of the family, of culture, and of social and political life. In this they look to the bishops for encouragement and leadership. The bishops' task in this regard is to promote the holiness of life and the Christian formation that will enable the laity, in the heart of the temporal order, 'to testify how the Christian faith constitutes the only fully valid response...to the problems and hopes that life poses to every person and society.' Exercising the discernment which belongs to your apostolic office, you must be like the 'householder who brings out of his treasure what is new and what is old.' It is in this sense that the new evangelization requires a renewal of pastoral governance and activity.

Throughout this speech—and his entire papacy—John Paul II never wavered in his support of clerical celibacy and strict, traditional sexual morality for all people. He never addressed the argument that this de-sexing of priests could be an underlying reason for the secret sexual activity in the Vatican, Ireland, and all over the globe.

So far, the Vatican has been able to avoid paying any price for the sexual abuses that have alienated so many of the people in Ireland and other countries, and cost so much in dollars and damaged lives. That may change. For the first time, a federal judge in the States has ruled that a sex-abuse lawsuit against the Vatican can proceed. U.S. District Judge Michael Mosman found enough of a connection between the Vatican and an abusing priest for him to be considered a Vatican employee. The implicit argument is that the pope appoints the bishops, who ordain and manage the priests, who commit the sexual atrocities (as do some bishops). The lawsuit claims that the "Holy See" was negligent in retaining Fr. Andrew Ronan in the priesthood, placing him in Portland, Oregon, failing to properly investigate or supervise him, and, finally, failing to warn of his sexual past.

Minnesota attorney Jeffrey Anderson, the premier legal advocate for abuse victims who brought the Ronan lawsuit, called it a "titanic legal victory" in the effort to hold the Vatican accountable for the international movement of predatory priests. In this case, Ronan admitted abusing boys in Ireland, was exported to the United States, and continued molesting boys in Chicago and in Portland. He has since died, but the lawsuit is very much alive. The case has the potential to make the papacy pay restitution for the abuses of its priests.[39] The Vatican was worried enough about the threat to ask U.S. Secretary of State Condoleezza Rice whether the U.S. government could stop a similar lawsuit in Kentucky. Rice said the Vatican had to fight the lawsuit itself. Recently, the church suffered a setback on that front, too, when a federal judge ruled that three men could pursue claims against the Vatican over allegations of sexual abuse by priests.[40]

The fact is that the Vatican, like any bureaucracy, has a limited ability to control the forces of change. Early in his papacy, the Polish Pope John Paul II looked to Ireland to support the traditional religiosity that was his own hallmark, but already then the Irish were shifting from the extremes of sexual repression to the extremes of sexual expression.

His successor, Pope Benedict XVI, went to Poland, where John Paul had helped drive out the "God-less" Communists, to make a similar case in that Catholic nation for traditional religious beliefs in a continent that had gone secular. Once again blaming outside pressures for the church's failings, Benedict urged the Polish people to resist the "wave of moral indifference and secularism washing across Europe." According to a Religion News Service dispatch, "He challenged Poles to bear the torch of Pope John Paul's legacy of conservative values and absolute truths with the same intensity that allowed them to turn the tide of the Cold War."[41] As John Paul once looked to Ireland, Benedict is looking to Poland to take the lead in bringing a resurgence of Christian values to a secular Europe. Alas, Polish Catholics were recently shaken by revelations that their priests and bishops had collaborated with the Communists.

Still, Benedict isn't giving up on Poland—or Ireland. In meeting with the Irish bishops in Rome, he called for them to help the people recognize the inability of the secular, materialistic culture to bring "true satisfaction and joy." Where will they find that joy? In following Christ and living according to his commandments, Benedict said.[42]

From what I saw in Ireland, however, many of the people are finding joy; not necessarily in following Christ, but in the materialism of a secular culture.

CHAPTER NINE

SHARED SECRETS

THE GOVERNOR AND THE PRIEST were good friends and understandably so; they shared an Irish heritage and the Roman Catholic
religion, as well as successful, satisfying careers. James McGreevey had risen
from mayor and legislator to be elected governor of New Jersey, and dreamed
of someday reaching the White House as president. Michael Cashman,
beloved as "Father Mike" by the people of his parish, had been named a
monsignor and gained prominence as a spiritual advisor to the governor.
He baptized one of McGreevey's two children, and had the honor of offering the benediction at the governor's inaugural.

But they also shared long-held secrets, dark secrets that would cripple,
if not destroy, their enviable careers. Cashman, who came from Ireland,
was the first to fall. Shortly after McGreevey took office, the priest was
accused of having sexually molested a mother and her two teenage children, a daughter and son. Though professing his innocence, he took a leave
of absence from his ministry.[1] Two years later, the Irish-American governor
McGreevey also resigned from his office, after admitting that as a married
man he had engaged in a homosexual affair with a male employee. "I am a
gay American," he said.[2]

I bring forth the sad stories of these two men because I believe they
illustrate a conclusion I have reached in this book: that the suppression of
sexual desire, followed by covert and destructive sexual expression, was an

127

underlying cause of the scandals that crippled not only the careers of these two men, but also their church. In Ireland it was a cultural celibacy born of a cataclysmic famine, as well as a strict clerical celibacy imposed by the Catholic Church. In America, it was a cultural celibacy and secrecy imposed on homosexuals, in addition to the demands of priestly celibacy imposed by the church—an American Catholic Church built in large part by Irish immigrants.

Fr. Cashman reacted to these strictures, I suggest, by allegedly imposing his sexual desires on the mother and her two children, not just once or twice, but over a period of several years. His attorney denied the allegations and predicted that Cashman would soon be exonerated and returned to his parish. It didn't happen. A church review board found that two allegations of sexual misconduct with a minor contained "at least a semblance of truth."[3] Even before that, the church had paid $145,000 to those alleged victims along with another woman who accused Cashman of "improper contact."[4] Earlier, Governor McGreevey had praised Cashman for his values and principles.

But Catholic values and principles posed a severe problem for McGreevey himself. McGreevey reacted to the repression of his homosexuality by engaging with scores of men in furtive, anonymous sex at rest stops, public parks and seedy bookstores. "I craved love," he perceptively admitted, "but sex was all that was available to me."[5] Later, during his rise in politics, he became an "avid womanizer," was married twice, and had two children—all of which provided a cover for his homosexuality. (He denied that he married his second wife for political reasons, saying "in my way I loved her. But as a gay man, I could only love her so much."[6])

After resigning from office, McGreevey contended that the Catholic Church's "pointlessly cruel war against gays and lesbians" helped drive him into self-denial and self-loathing—even into thoughts of suicide. He said he couldn't live up to the sexual norms of the church, which put him into a posture of dishonesty from the time he was in the eighth grade, when he first became aware he was sexually different. He was made to believe that a supposedly "loving God" had condemned him to a life of suffering.[7]

In his last year of high school, however, the devout McGreevey believed that the Catholic priesthood, through its celibacy requirement, might solve what he then considered to be the problem of his homosexual orientation. Such a vocation might be easier for gays than straights, he thought, because gays were already practiced in denial. He was encouraged in this thinking by the fact he felt that some good, honorable priests he knew were homosexuals, including the young priest from Ireland who recommended the priesthood for him. The Irish priest, he said, seemed to suggest that the priesthood would enable him to turn away from his "evil" sexual drive and toward the good of community service and God.[8] While McGreevey ultimately decided against going to seminary, his reasons for considering the priesthood may have been shared by many other gays, helping to explain why so many of them have become priests.

By offering the stories of the governor and the priest, I am not saying that celibacy, whether imposed by society or the Catholic Church, is the sole or even major cause of sexual abuse in Ireland and America. Some experts on such matters contend that it is not a factor at all. I am not an expert, but I feel that the facts I have gathered in my years of research strongly suggest that this repression of sex helps to explain why so many priests, especially Irish priests, contributed, through their abuse, to the greatest scandal in the history of the modern church. I am not alone in this belief. As I noted in Chapter Seven, experts in the Irish government's Ferns report unanimously agreed that celibacy contributed to the abuse problem. Similarly, Donal Leader of the Irish Christian Brothers said he found some truth in the argument that if sexuality is repressed, it is bound to find some form of expression, sometimes deviant and criminal. And Irish Bishop Willie Walsh expressed the opinion that either the extreme of repression or the extreme of wide-open sexuality "is going to lead to some destructive forms of abuse of sexuality." Leader and Walsh have both seen the extreme of repression in their country, accompanied by widespread sexual misconduct in the Christian Brothers and in the priesthood.

Of course, celibacy can't be the only underlying cause of clergy sex abuse. Sexual deviance was a problem long before the Catholic Church made a concerted effort to enforce clerical celibacy in the twelfth century, after centuries of sporadic and failed efforts. While attorneys and advocates for victims, as well as the news media, have brought to public attention today the terrible scourge of abuse, Catholic priests and bishops didn't suddenly become abusive in modern times. As I have pointed out, and as documented in *Sex, Priests and Secret Codes*, they have been accused of sexual misconduct for centuries. This book provides compelling evidence that "objectionable and criminal" child abuse by the clergy has been a recurring and widespread problem throughout the entire 2,000-year history of the church. Moreover, according to the authors, Thomas P. Doyle, A. W. Richard Sipe, and Patrick J. Wall, church leaders for a long time have conspired to silence the victims and protect the perpetrators.

> Many people, Catholics included, have been shocked to rediscover within the last decades just how prevalent clerical misbehavior is. Abuse, however, is not a new phenomenon. Sexual activity by popes, bishops, and priests—members of the ruling hierarchy bound to celibacy—has triggered every reform the church has been forced to undergo. The rape and sodomy of children is woven into the tradition of clerical history. And it has been amply recorded in documents and literature.[9]

It is appropriate to ask: why didn't church leaders act to prevent this blatant sexual activity once they imposed mandatory celibacy? The answer, Doyle and his colleagues write, is that the Catholic authorities have defended the "ideal" in theory, but they have failed to maintain it in practice. The authors describe how the church not only failed to protect children, but tolerated the abuse of vulnerable women under the myth that the women were to blame for their own abuse. Beyond committing abuse, the authors note, even more priests, many more, have been sexually involved with men and women, acceptably under civil law but not church law. The undeniable reality, they say, is that celibacy has not worked in the past, and does not work today, for what may well be a majority of clerics.[10] Sipe, a married priest and expert on sexuality in the clergy, states in his preface that the inability of the church to enforce the obligations of celibacy, coupled with the elitist and secret club mentality that it fosters, contribute to a climate that allows child abuse to happen.[11]

Sipe writes in another book that "the more sexuality was outlawed, the more it flourished." He gives the example of Pope Julius III (1550–1555), who had a homosexual involvement with a 15-year-old boy whom he named a cardinal. And in the same century, Pope Pius IV was the father of three children.[12] Another critic, Peter De Rosa, puts it bluntly: "After six centuries of strenuous efforts to impose celibacy, the clergy were a menace to the wives and young women of the parishes to which they were sent."[13] If you think the situation in Ireland and America today is bad, consider Spain in the 1700s and 1800s. Priests in confession, says De Rosa, were soliciting nuns, children, and adults for sex, even engaging in sex right there in the confessional.[14] Nor were the Spanish priests any worse than clergy in other countries, says De Rosa.

> Too many clerics were forced to lead an unnatural life. They were probably well intentioned when they offered themselves for ordination. If they became corrupt, it was because enforced celibacy corrupted them. They were the first victims of a papal system that ignored the apostle's warning: "It is better to marry than to burn (with passion)."[15]

I have reported how the Irish priests and bishops, in their country and America, became corrupted within the bonds of celibacy, both cultural and religious. Did imposed celibacy cause the corruption? I make my case for this primarily on the startlingly high rate of sexual abuse within the Irish society at large under the straightjacket of cultural celibacy. It appears that many Irish men, thus limited in normal sexual activity, gave vent to their desires in deviant behavior, some as a result of having been abused themselves. Many of these men also expressed their sexuality in secret under the cloak of celibacy in the priesthood. Cause and effect? Donal Leader of the Christian Brothers, Bishop Walsh, and the experts in the Ferns inquiry all suggest a direct connection.

However, Andrew Greeley, the prominent Chicago priest, sociologist, and novelist, argues forcefully against this cause and effect as applied to the abuse of children. In *Memories of a Parish Priest*, he writes:

> Pedophilia is not caused by celibacy. It is an obsession acquired very early in life and is apparently incurable. Most pedophiles are married men. If the pedophile priests were permitted to marry, they would continue to prey on children, often their own. One can perhaps make a case for the reform of the celibacy discipline, but pedophilia is not an appropriate argument for those who seek such reform. Quite the contrary, it is an intellectually dishonest if not bigoted response, equally so when advanced by Catholic "liberals."[16]

The outspoken Greeley speaks in absolutes. However, if pedophilia is an acquired obsession, as he claims, I submit that the cultural celibacy I have described in Ireland helped Oliver O'Grady—and probably many other men—learn to be a pedophile in a cycle of abuse. Two priests and a brother, themselves products of a sexually repressive culture, unleashed their sexual desires on young Oliver, who then abused his sister and went on as a priest to continue a career of abuse in America. Most experts would agree with an explanation like this, though there are no data to prove it.

A minority of experts suggest that some men (or priests) might have been genetically predisposed to be pedophiles. Some of these flawed men may have viewed the priesthood as an opportunity to prey on children, but others could have believed that celibacy would help them overcome their perverted compulsions. As we saw in the case of teenager James McGreevey, young men who feel that they have deviant sexual desires, even if not involving children, sometimes look to the priesthood as a means of avoidance.

In making my case for the role of celibacy in the abuse scandal, furthermore, I am addressing more than pedophilia, or the abuse of children. I'm also considering the abuse of teenagers and adults, both women and men. Cultural and clerical celibacy likely played a part in those types of abuse, which were widely practiced in Irish society and in the priesthood.

In my quest for causes, however, I initially thought that cultural celibacy in Ireland, born of the great famine, would have faded away long ago. I was wrong. Amazingly, it persisted into modern times, as shown in a 1959 article in the *Clare Champion* newspaper of Ennis. Under the headline, "The Fewness and Lateness of Marriages in Ireland," an official of the St. Patrick's College seminary in Carlow was quoted saying, "There must be something fundamentally wrong when the normal vigour of youth is so often prepared to forego marriage for non-serious economic reasons, or for selfish personal reasons, and when parents so often stubbornly decide to consign son or daughter to a prolonged life of bachelorhood or spinsterhood."

While decrying "selfish personal reasons" for avoiding marriage, Fr. R. Prendergast, vice-president of the college, acknowledged that many men didn't have adequate income to support families. I visited Ireland in the 1950s and can vouch for the poverty. It was a poverty that helped account for the fact that Ireland at that time had the lowest marriage rate in the world, according to author Fintan O'Toole.

Michael Kenny is a striking example of the sexually stunted priests who came out of the repressive Irish culture of the 1950s and 1960s to break loose in America. As I described him in Chapter Three, Kenny admitted being involved in sexual activity with 10 women, including the fathering of two children. Now consider his background. One of seven children in a poor farm family, lacking a father at home after age ten, he went to an all-boys boarding school, never experiencing any adolescent infatuation with a girl. He woke up sexually in the priesthood, first with a teenager of 17, the normal age for high-school dating. Kenny was 29 or 30 at the time, as he remembered it. From then, he went on to engage in sexual intercourse with six women, and to have intimate relationships with four others, most of them young, some on the rebound from divorces or a breakup. All the sex, he said, was consensual, though he felt guilty after the first time.

We are talking about high school behavior here— Kenny going with the young women to movies and restaurants on dates, dancing, buying drinks for two minors in a bar, coming home late, but still finding time to be a practicing priest. His "parent" in his first seven years as a priest was a permissive pastor and friend who professed to see nothing, hear nothing, and know nothing about his associate's sexual activity. As you might guess, the pastor, Thomas Flanagan, also came from Ireland, as did a high percentage of the other priests in the San Antonio, Texas, archdiocese. Flanagan apparently maintained control of his sexuality; he would later be named a bishop. But Kenny was out of control, and emotionally unprepared for the dating game. When one of the young women jilted him after a five-year affair, he went into a psychiatric hospital in deep depression, had trouble eating and sleeping, broke out crying, thought of suicide. It was a learning experience. Kenny recovered and continued his sexual adventures, until two of the women brought complaints against him and the church, costing him his career and prompting him to return to Ireland. By that time, Ireland had abandoned the cultural celibacy that formed his life, but Kenny, living with a sister, said he had nothing more to do with sex.[17]

Kenny had joined the priesthood as a way out of poverty and to please his mother. He had a heterosexual problem. Other young Irish men, with homosexual identity problems, became priests thinking celibacy would help them submerge their sexual desires, as James McGreevey considered doing. They joined the priesthood not to prey on altar boys and choirgirls, but through celibacy to keep from doing so. Journalists Elinor Burkett and Frank Bruni, in their book *A Gospel of Shame*, quote a minister saying that some men and women feel that "the mere act of ordination would trigger a mystical transformation that would lift their desires." Burkett and Bruni continue:

True pedophiles usually begin to feel this attraction at an early age—more than half before they turn eighteen, according to one study. Despite popular portrayals of such people as depraved perverts without any semblance of conscience, many are actually ashamed of, and frightened by, what they feel. Some repress it far below conscious awareness. Others knowingly struggle to buck their impulses. If a man with these feelings is Catholic, and religious, entering the celibate culture of the priesthood seems like a perfect defense—a commitment to holiness that promises to keep the demons at bay.[18]

Were the demons kept at bay? Many were; some were not. If these authors are right, and I think they are, the dominant church in Ireland would attract a lot of potential abusers—not just pedophiles, but also the men more likely to abuse teenagers and adults. These are the men who, like Kenny, were deprived of any awareness of sexuality in their youth and, lacking emotional maturity, were attracted sexually as priests to the teenagers and young adults with whom they identified. These are the men, also, who might have the propensity to over-use alcohol, which would release their inhibitions and cause them to act out their sexual desires. Ireland, of course, had no monopoly on these emotionally dwarfed men, but because so many in that country were Catholic, and so many of them went into the priesthood, it had a disproportionate supply of potential abusers. And many of them went to the United States.

As I've admitted, I cannot prove conclusively that sexual repression and imposed celibacy directly lead to clergy sex abuse. In fact, when I discussed my hypothesis with two brothers in my cradle-Catholic family of 13 children, they scoffed at my lack of any scientific, controlled studies to prove it. However, staging such a study seems impossible: how could researchers convince a large sample of priests to participate in an experiment to see how many would become abusers and why?

Neither can I prove that the celibate priesthood attracts more men with sexual problems than does the married ministry of other religions. Stephen

Rossetti, a priest, psychologist, and president of the St. Luke Institute which treats priestly abusers, agrees that "some people with sexual problems seek out a celibate lifestyle in an unconscious attempt to escape their own sexuality." But he cautions against making any generalizations from such anecdotal information. As for whether priests are more likely to be abusers than others in society, he gives the short answer: "We don't know."

One thing I know is that there will be no studies on this matter coming out of the church, not under its present policies. Fr. Donald Cozzens, an authority on the priesthood, laments the failure to address the issue. "To insist that there is simply no correlation between mandatory celibacy and the present crisis over clergy misconduct with minors looks like bureaucratic bullying, as long as the Vatican remains opposed to even discussion concerning the systems undergirding the priestly lifestyle."[19] Strong language, yes. But I talked to Father Cozzens after reading his book, *The Changing Face of the Prietshood*, and he struck me as a reasonable priest who would not use such language unless it was justified.

The Catholic Church, with its demand for sexless men, has lost its grip on Ireland, partly as a result of the abuses it engendered and tolerated. The poverty-driven celibate culture, which kept men from marrying and, as I see it, led to so much abuse in society, has receded in a wave of prosperity. The Irish church is left dealing with the cost and the shame of what was wrought by its chosen clerics when they broke loose from the sexual repression of years past. Now, in a sexually open society, the church might find it even more difficult to enforce clerical celibacy.

When I started the research for this book, I felt that the Irish Catholic Church would offer a microcosm of the sex abuse scandal and might portend the future for the American church. After all, this tiny country has often had an out-sized influence on the bigger world stage, from religion to literature and from American culture to guerilla warfare. Yes, Irish hero Michael Collins developed a style of warfare that drove out the British and is still followed today around the world. But the more recent "enemy" has not been an alien force, but an enemy within.

Maybe the Irish church fell so rapidly, losing its power and prestige, because it was once so powerful and rigid. When cracks appeared, it shattered like a window pane. The church may eventually overcome its scandals and regain its strong presence in Irish life. Or it may continue to stumble, like its once-popular Bishop Casey, who returned from exile to lose his driver's license over drunk driving and to lose his priestly privileges, pending a Vatican inquiry, after being accused of long-ago child abuse.

Perhaps the American church, more diverse and less rigid, will be more resilient. Who can say? I won't try to predict, based on Ireland's example, whether the American church will weather the sex-abuse storm and emerge stronger, or limp along permanently impaired. History will provide the final answer.

I have discussed in this chapter the stories of James McGreevey and Michael Cashman to examine the role of celibacy, cultural and clerical, in the Catholic sex abuse scandal. Beyond that, I propose that their cases put in stark relief the dilemma for the church in trying to deal with another contentious issue—homosexuality in the priesthood. And that truly is a huge issue. An estimated one-third of the priests are homosexual, and fully two thirds of the abuse cases counted by the church in its 2004 study involved male priests and boys.

The Vatican's response to those abusive gay relationships has been to order a ban on any candidates for the priesthood who are actively homosexual or have deep-seated homosexual tendencies, as well as those who support the "so-called gay culture."[20] McGreevey might have been excluded from the priesthood on those grounds, though he had no propensity to be an abuser of boys. Or, he could have been accepted as a priest if he had kept secret his sexual preferences.

In targeting homosexuals, however, the Vatican has failed to address the fact that many of the abusing priests, like Cashman, have been heterosexual, especially those from Ireland as I have documented in this narrative. Cashman, accused of molesting a girl and boy and their mother, might not have been subjected to special scrutiny for the priesthood, since he had a propensity to be an abuser across sexual lines.

Understandably, church leaders find it difficult to decide how much to blame gays for the sex-abuse scandal and how to weed out potential abusers. One Vatican official denied any scapegoating of homosexuals and noted that being gay does not mean being a pedophile, or having an adult attraction to children. But, he added, "The church had a responsibility to be sure that adolescent males in its care are not at risk from homosexual priests who are not chaste."[21]

I would say that the preponderance of male-to-male abuse in the American church certainly justifies the assertion of that responsibility. The Vatican official acknowledged that sexually active heterosexual priests also are a risk, but he said the risk is greater for gay clergy because they are more likely to have unsupervised contact with adolescent males than with females.

As I have pointed out, however, many of the heterosexual priests from Ireland, including Michael Cashman, have had no trouble finding girls to abuse, whether in schools, youth groups, or—as in Cashman's case—in their homes. So, as I see it, the challenge for church officials is how to carry out their protective responsibility without just singling out homosexuals, as the Vatican seems to be doing.

James McGreevey, meantime, has renewed his teenage desire to be a priest—this time in the Episcopal church, which has no ban on men who are actively homosexual or support the gay lifestyle. In fact, the church has consecrated a bishop with that background, and, accordingly, has accepted McGreevey in one of its seminaries.

CHAPTER TEN

An Epilogue
and More

FTER YEARS OF WORK on this book, I thought I had seen it all. Those broken Irish priests, from abusive or repressive backgrounds, had acted out their pent-up sexual desires in America through their perverted abuses of girls, boys, young men, and women. In so doing, they helped cripple their church—a church now beset by bankruptcies, reeling from massive abuse payments, and depleted by the self-destruction of its priests. Though my research came to an end, the scandal did not—and will not.

Two news events, on opposite ends of America, showed that the Irish tragedy has no final act. In Florida, two Irish priests were accused of stealing almost $9 million from the church and spending it on girlfriends, gambling, boozing, international travel, expensive homes, and investments.[1] And in California, a bishop filed for bankruptcy protection, thus delaying payments to abuse victims and averting release of information on accusations of his own sexual misconduct long past. In that one, a lawsuit involving an Irish priest, among others, was put on hold, prompting the alleged victim to attack the bishop for thwarting her quest for redress. Her response illustrates the vital role that abuse survivors are playing in this story.[2]

These two cases highlight added dimensions of the clergy scandal, beyond what I've presented in this book. According to the allegations, the two Irish priests in Florida displayed an insatiable greed for money along with a continuing quest for sex, for men coming from what was then a poor country where money and sex were scarce. What better place to find both than in Florida, the reputed haven for hedonism in affluent America? The California case portrays the amazing and admirable persistence of one woman over almost two decades, seeking to make her alleged abuser and his church pay for their crimes.

The Catholic Church and its faithful followers were the main victims of the two priests in Florida; they lost a huge amount of money and suffered a staggering blow to their reputation. According to investigators, Fr. John Skehan enriched himself for four decades as pastor at St. Vincent Ferrer Catholic Church in Delray Beach. His successor, Fr. Frank Guinan, had less time to fill his pockets from the collection plate, but he was working at it until they were both caught and charged with grand theft.

Meantime, the women in this story reaped the rewards of their romantic relationships, the priests giving them tens of thousands of dollars, paying their credit card bills, taking them to gambling resorts and, in one case, even to Ireland. But their story didn't end there.

One of the women, Colleen Duffey (now a married adult), told of her tangled relationship with Fr. Skehan, a hard-drinking man from Ireland's County Kilkenny. Colleen, then 15 years old, was hired to work for Skehan's church, where she became his personal assistant, and more. Colleen administered eye drops, took him to the doctor, picked up prescriptions, arranged plane trips, drove him to the airport and back, and even took him home from the pub when he had too much to drink. Colleen was also the private sexual fantasy of this priest, 50 years her senior. Skehan lusted after her for years, Duffey said, and hugged and kissed her "all the time."

"I believed the man wanted me sexually," Colleen later said, "because he would tell me all the time, 'I love you, but I don't want you to think that I want you sexually.'" Skehan had to be careful as a priest, but he was less careful under the influence alcohol, when he took Colleen out to dinner. Then he would tell her she was the most beautiful woman, and if he were younger he would want her and take care of her. He wished he wasn't so old. People in the restaurant, he would say, thought he was dating a beautiful woman. Skehan was living out the private fantasies of an aging priest. On her part, Colleen would tell him she was flattered, but she kept the priest at bay.

One time in Ireland, Skehan lost control. While Colleen and a friend were staying with his family, Skehan went into a jealous rage over her friendship with his nephew. That's when "he made advances towards me," she said, emphasizing that she didn't let him go beyond that. Another time, the priest took hold of her as if to strangle her, again in a drunken outburst of jealousy. Colleen's relationship with the priest went cold after that, but he kept apologizing, wanting to be closer once more, until she finally forgave him and things went back to the way they were.

Colleen's mother knew about the relationship. She told her that the priest's feelings seemed to be "more than grandfather love," but her mother did not intervene. She understood that kind of behavior because she'd seen her share of alcoholism in her own family. Asked whether she didn't expect different behavior from a priest, the mother answered, "A man's a man, I suppose." Besides, she trusted him as a friend of the family. As I found in so many other cases, that familial feeling about Irish priests, especially by Irish girls and women, helped explain why so many of them got away with so much, over and over.

Throughout her narrative of her sexually-charged relationship with Skehan, Colleen never expressed any thought that she was a victim. After all, he helped her buy a new car, took her out to restaurants, went drinking with her in pubs, and sent her flowers and greeting cards to show his feelings for her. Fr. Skehan was the man "I loved and trusted," she said. Many other women involved with Irish priests have said much the same.

But in addition to his unfulfilled love for Colleen, Skehan allegedly had a sexual affair with one of his long-time employees. More than that, a man was said to have caught and photographed the priest in bed with his wife. (It's all in the prosecutor's files.) But this was hardly anything new in the paradise Palm Beach diocese; remember my accounts of the priestly sexual activities there of native Irishmen Frank Flynn and Matthew Fitzgerald.

Still, Palm Beach wasn't all paradise for the women involved with these priests. Carol Hagen told investigators that her involvement with Fr. Guinan, lasting only a couple of years, was "no great love affair, trust me." Maybe so, but he paid her $47,000 in one 10-month period, after she said the affair had ended. Skehan was more generous, shelling out $122,175 to his friend, the late Hilda Nataline. Love affairs with priests can be profitable, however fraught with danger.

Where were the bishops, the enforcers of churchly law and order, when all this was going on? It is worth mentioning again that two of the Palm Beach bishops, J. Keith Symons and Irishman Anthony O'Connell, had been compromised themselves by their previous sexual abuse of boys.

Like Colleen Duffey and Carol Hagen in Florida, Nicki Rister in California has talked openly about her past relationship with a priest from Ireland (see Chapter Two). It's the willingness of many such women, after years of silence, to finally speak about the sexual activities of these priests that makes it impossible for me to write a truly final chapter for this book. More and more of them are stepping forward, overcoming secrecy and shame to keep the story going. They are going public in lawsuits, criminal investigations, and interviews. Some, like Duffey, speak out even though they are not seeking redress. Others, like Rister, are pursuing legal action to obtain compensation for alleged abuse. More than money, however, the record in many cases shows they want the church to be held accountable for what they suffered.

Rister, for example, has fought for years, not for compensation but for vindication, going first to her bishop, then to the police, and finally to a civil lawsuit when all else failed. Later she traveled to Dublin to confront her alleged abuser, Fr. Patrick O'Keeffe, when he was questioned by attorneys. Then she went to San Diego, California, for the trial, which was the first of many cases to be heard, only to suffer the disappointment of further delay. Under bankruptcy protection obtained by the church, the lawsuits would be held in abeyance while a negotiated settlement was sought on the damage claims.

On the very day the church announced plans to file for bankruptcy, Rister issued a statement vowing to continue her fight. "What I perceive to be lies and hiding and meaningless apologies reinforce my desire to see my case through to the end," she said. "I plan on being the eternal thorn in the Catholic Church's side." That was no empty rhetoric. Right away, she went to the court files and found that when the San Diego bishop, Robert Brom, filed for bankruptcy, he not only stopped the lawsuits, he also warded off a demand that he produce documents on a church investigation into the sex-abuse allegations against him. Brom and other bishops had been accused of joining in a sexual orgy at a seminary in southern Minnesota. Brom also was alleged to have forced oral sex on a seminarian.

The relentless Rister—and attorneys for other abuse victims—concluded that Brom had filed for bankruptcy protection partly to prevent the release of those investigative documents. It is true that Brom had refused earlier to release them when Rister's attorney demanded them, but whether that partly accounts for his bankruptcy filing is a question. The bishop said he decided to go into bankruptcy because damage awards, if early trials proceeded, could deplete church resources and leave nothing for other victims.

Ever the thorn in the church's side, Rister commented, "Bishop Brom let it slip that there had been an investigation of him, himself, his excellency, the robed holy one himself—about taking part in 'this specific orgy at the seminary,' like there were a lot of them?" Before the bankruptcy filing, she said, the church had been losing its battle to withhold documents in its "own corporate personnel files regarding sexual misconduct of the church's own hierarchy." Actually, Brom didn't let it slip. In fact, according to newspaper reports, Brom had said some time ago that such an investigation had disproved the allegations against him. I would argue, though, that the church would help its credibility by releasing the reports of its inquiries, especially when it investigates itself. On the contrary, I've found that it routinely refuses to do so in sexual misconduct cases involving bishops. The typical response of the church: take our word for it, found to be not guilty. Considering the church's extensive record of deception, however, Rister had good reason for wanting to see those documents.

Rister, along with the other abuse survivors, prevailed. Near the end of 2007, in the midst of the bankruptcy proceedings, the church agreed to a settlement calling for payment of nearly $200 million to the 144 people who said they were sexually abused by Catholic priests in the San Diego diocese. The church also agreed to release internal documents in the abuse cases, as sought by Rister and the others. Said Bishop Brom, "I'm very, very sorry for the suffering we have caused them." I would add that the church also is suffering. The settlement brings the total amount it must pay to abuse victims in the nation to $2.3 billion, and more is sure to come.

Even then, despite the ever rising costs, the Vatican remains partly in denial. Just recently, after Catholic authorities had been accused for years of trying to cover up the endemic sex abuses, and after the Irish and American churches themselves had finally laid out the scope of the scandal, a Vatican official, while admitting the gravity of the allegations, declared that heavy coverage of the abuses by the mass media must be denounced because it "discredits the church."

As I have shown in this narrative, and as the recent San Diego settlement demonstrates, it is not the news media but the bishops and priests—including many Irish priests, like O'Keeffe—who are responsible for the mounting costs and human suffering of this unending tragedy of the Catholic Church.

AFTERWORD

M OST OF THE SEXUAL ABUSE CASES I examined for this book were wrenching, but I was almost never personally touched by them. I knew only one priest accused of misconduct, and none of the victims. Then, at the very end, I was stunned to learn that one of the priestly abusers was a boyhood friend, a member of my youth softball team, a like-minded guy I enjoyed visiting with in the following years, and a generous friend who loaded me up with grapes from the arbor at his home in retirement. When he died prematurely after that last visit, I grieved the loss of Martin Senko, a man I considered to be a dedicated priest, even though he was known to be abrasive and unbending, traits that kept him from advancing in the clerical ranks. He certainly was not the only priest, or friend, to suffer from those character flaws.

However, in mid-2007, when the Catholic archdiocese of Portland, Oregon, released information on a number of its errant priests, the Martin Senko I knew was among them. According to 10 pages of documentation, Martin had sexually abused a female student for four years in the 1960s at the Catholic high school where he was a teacher and principal. I was jarred to read how that abuse affected the girl, as described by clergy vicar Charles Lienert after he met with her. "She has a lot of guilt about it and blamed herself because she needed attention," he wrote in a letter for the file. "It's only in recent years that she has come to realize through therapy that it was not her fault, although she still has a lot of emotion about it. . . . She felt she was trapped at the time and that her only escape was graduation." Even then, according to Lienert, Fr. Senko made it difficult for her to get into college because of the recommendation she needed from the school to get a scholarship."

That was not the end of it. For years thereafter Martin tried frequently to reestablish the relationship, making a seeming apology in one letter, but mostly he demonstrated his narcissism, expressing his needs and how he would love to be able to share with her. She rebuffed him and finally told vicar Lienert about it more than two decades later, in the early 1990s, when she was encouraged to come forward after the therapy because of rumors he had abused other women. This young woman was not seeking money in a lawsuit; on the contrary, she said she didn't want to get Fr. Senko in trouble and expressed the hope her testimony might be useful in getting help for him.

Upon learning of the demons bedeviling Martin, I recalled how he had reprimanded my wife one time about the temptation she presented when wearing red leotards, and how he later told me I was exaggerating the problem of sexual abuse in the church. Of course, he didn't tell me that he was part of the problem, though he had already admitted as much to Fr. Lienert, claiming the student relationship consisted only of "touching." He didn't tell me, either, that he also had engaged in sexual affairs with adult women.

This account is of more than personal interest. It involves a classic case of cover-up; the girl told two other priests about the abuse while it was happening, but they apparently did nothing to stop it. Twenty-four years later, when Archbishop William Levada was informed of that abuse and a lesser allegation, he sent Martin to treatment but kept the matter secret and allowed him to continue as a parish priest. It was a typical case all the way through. The archbishop excused years of sexual abuse, assured by therapists that Martin's "issues" had been addressed in treatment. At one point,

Lienert suggested to the archbishop that "a supportive note from you would be very helpful to Father Senko." No mention was made of his victim.

Martin's case also is significant because his bishop, Levada, is now the pope's enforcer of the faith, responsible for handling sex-abuse cases for the entire church. Will he do better in that job than he did in dealing with Martin and other priests in similar circumstances? He claims that his knowledge of the "terrible issue" will help him make sure that "these things are handled in the proper manner." Indeed, in his new role and with the backing of a new pope, Levada has disciplined two prominent priests for sexual misconduct, showing a resolve lacking before. Perhaps he has learned his lesson.

I cite this case not because it involves an Irish priest; it does not. Rather, I use it to close this book because it shows that all humans have weaknesses and failings, Irish or not, strangers or friends. And it illustrates once again how the lordly, all-powerful bishops, rather than dealing with these human failings, allowed them to grow and fester into the worst scandal in the history of the American church. The Irish priests and bishops played a major role in all this, but I do not intend to put the onus only on the Irish. Thousands of other priests and many bishops, like Martin Senko and William Levada, also played their parts in the scandal and evaded responsibility. Yes, that has begun to change; priests are being held responsible, but not their bishops. Under church policy today, my friend Martin would have been barred from performing as a priest after his misconduct was brought to light. But the new policy, imposed by the bishops themselves, does little to make accountable those church leaders who, like Martin's bishop, fail to protect vulnerable members of their flock from the priests who would violate them.

And so, through this painful personal account of a friend, I bring to a close this story, untold until now, of how Irish priests, the backbone and soul of the American Catholic Church, helped to cripple that church, the church they built.

Acknowledgments

AMONG THE MANY PEOPLE who helped me produce this book, I could thank my spouse Jan for her support and encouragement, as so many authors do in a rather token fashion. But I will go beyond that to give Jan credit for offering a suggestion that would make this a different and, I think, much better kind of book. Write a narrative, she said, that would include my personal experiences, opinions and reflections as a birth Catholic. So that's what I did, relying on her knowledge as a reader of almost a book a day for many decades. As a one-time author of a newspaper column, "You and Your Children," and as a prodigious letter-writer, Jan writes as well as reads.

As for my research on clergy sex abuse, I owe a special debt to two of the most indefatigable advocates I have ever known. Richard Sipe, a married priest, and Father Tom Doyle, both preeminent clergy-abuse experts, have testified in hundreds of court cases, written books, and challenged the church time after time on behalf of abuse survivors. Busy as they are, they have assisted me throughout the five years I have worked on this issue, first involving Catholic bishops, then regarding Irish priests. Through meetings and e-mails, they've told me of abusers, suggested sources and answered countless queries, never flagging in their help despite my failure for so long to get into print and justify the use of their time.

I am also especially thankful for the help of Catholic historian Terry Dosh and BishopAccountability.org's Anne Barrett Doyle. Terry met with me many times to discuss my research and findings, while Anne provided rare access to her organization's amazingly comprehensive archive of clergy sexual abuse and cover-up cases.

Where do I stop? Certainly not before I mention the generous assistance of the many attorneys who represent abuse survivors. Most of them went out of their way to provide documents, convince clients to talk to me and advise of pertinent cases. Over those five years, that's the help I received from Jeffrey Anderson, the dean of attorneys on abuse cases, along with attorneys Tim Kosnoff, Michael Pfau, Sylvia Demarest, John Manly, Tahira Khan Merritt, Ray Mouton, Timothy Conlon and J. Douglas Sutter. Patrick Wall, a senior consultant with the Manly & McGuire law firm, also provided considerable assistance.

In fact, almost everyone I approached responded generously. In Europe and America, that includes journalistic colleagues John L. Allen Jr., John Thavis, Austin Hobbs, Jason Berry, Seamus O'Reilly, Robert Blair Kaiser, Guillermo Contreras, Sam Hemingway and Robert Mickens. It includes priests Tony Flannery, Kevin Clinton, Peter Schonenbach, and Joseph Starmann. It also includes sociologist William Smith, abuse survivors Nicki Rister, Susan Renehan, Mark Brooks, and Michael Wegs, as well as my long-time friend and lawyer-consultant Fred Granata and my European translators and researchers Christoph Becker and Sylvia Schliebe. Christoph and Sylvia spent countless days finding, translating and evaluating documents on the abuse case involving Cardinal Groer in Austria; then were gracious and helpful hosts when my wife and I visited them in Germany.

All this could have been for naught. Publishers and literary agents rejected or failed to respond to my many inquiries, telling me that my subject was no longer of much interest to the American public. Author Lee Podles was not deterred by this response; he felt the full scope of the historic Catholic scandal should be brought to light. To help do so, he started Crossland Press, first to publish his book, *Sacrilege: Sexual Abuse in the Catholic Church*, an account of biblical proportions, and then to add my book as a companion work. And to prepare my book for publication, he assigned Sam Torode to do the editing, and what a great choice. Through careful attention to organization and detail, Sam helped make the book the best it could be.

Thanks to you all.

Endnotes

INTRODUCTION

1. Flannery, Tony. *From the Inside: A Priest's Views of the Catholic Church.* Dublin: Mercier Press, 1999. Other information comes from an interview by the author in Clarinbridge, County Galway, Ireland, on September 21, 2004.
2. Cahill, Thomas. *How the Irish Saved Civilization.* New York: Anchor Books, 1995.
3. "All Hallows Pioneer Priests in the United States," a booklet provided by All Hallows College (Dublin, Ireland), pp. 33-34.

PROLOGUE

1. The documentation on O'Connell in this summary section will be cited in detail in subsequent chapters.
2. John Jay College of Criminal Justice of the City University of New York, "The Prevalence of Sexual Abuse of Children by Priests," U.S. Conference of Catholic Bishops, 2004, pp. 16, 57. This original study reported that since 1950 more than 4,000 priests abused 10,400 minors. Since that study was released, the church in the following four years received additional allegations that brought the total to more than 6,000 priests and almost 14,000 victims. (Center for Applied Research in the Apostolate, 2007 survey of allegations and costs, a summary report for the Office of Child Protection, United States Conference of Catholic Bishops, February 2008, Washington, D.C.)
3. Press release, October 28, 2006, of the address of Pope Benedict XVI to the Irish bishops, the Catholic Communications Office of the Irish Bishops' Conference, Dublin, Ireland.

CHAPTER ONE: AN IRISH PEDOPHILE

1. Deposition of Oliver O'Grady in Tipperary, Ireland, March 30-31, 2005. The information in this chapter comes from the deposition except as otherwise cited in footnotes.
2. Curtis, Kim. "Former Priest Reveals Lifetime of Abuse and Offending," The Associated Press, June 5, 2005.
3. This estimate is based on a sample of 65 Irish-born priests accused of abuse in the United States, collected by the author from various sources.
4. Goode, Helen, Hannah McGee, and Ciaran O'Boyle. *Time to Listen: Confronting Child Sexual Abuse by Catholic Clergy in Ireland.* Dublin: The Liffey Press, 2003, p.10.
5. *Psychology Today*'s Diagnosis Dictionary: Pedophilia (http://psychologytoday.com/conditions/pedophilia.html).
6. Russell, Ron. "Mouth Wide Shut," *New Times* (Los Angeles), April 18, 2002.
7. O'Grady deposition and Russell.
8. Ibid.
9. Flannery, *From the Inside*, pp. 178-179.
10. "Oregon's Accused Clergy Since 1985," *The Oregonian* (Portland), July 7, 2002.
11. *Psychology Today.*
12. Russell.
13. Ibid.
14. Letter from Father Gerald Fitzgerald of New Mexico to unidentified archbishop, September 18, 1957, and letter from Archbishop James Davis of Santa Fe, NM, to Fitzgerald, August 23, 1965.
15. The Congregation for Catholic Education, "Concerning the Criteria of Vocational Discernment Regarding Persons with Homosexual Tendencies in View of Their Admission to Seminaries and Holy Orders." (The Vatican, November 4, 2005.)
16. Piccalo, Gina. ""Film Keeps Focus on Pedophile Priest," *Los Angeles Times*, February 17, 2007.

CHAPTER TWO: PRIESTS AND CHILDREN

1. Smith, William L. *Irish Priests in the United States.* Lanham, MD: University Press of America, 2004, p.109.
2. Letter from Father James O'Malley in County Mayo, Ireland, to Bishop Charles White of Spokane, WA, July 1, 1943.
3. Smith, p. 109.
4. de Leon, Virginia. "Lawsuit Claims Diocese Knew Priest Was Pedophile," *The Spokesman Review* (Spokane, WA), July 10, 2003.
5. The information on Father O'Doherty comes from the *Watertown Daily Times* (Watertown, NY), in articles from March 24 to December 9, 2002, and from the *Press Republican* (Ogdensburg, NY), January 31, 2003.
6. Letter from Bishop White to J. J. Conway, president of St. Patrick's College, Carlow, Ireland, June 26, 1946.
7. Letter from Bishop White to Conway, September 10, 1942.

8. Tu, Janet, "Spokane Diocese Agrees to Pay at least $48 million to Settle Clergy Abuse," *Seattle Times* (Seattle, WA), January 4, 2007.

9. The author's estimate on the percentage of Irish-born priests accused of sex abuse is based primarily on a sample of 716 priests from Carlow College in Ireland who came to the United States between 1950 and 1993. See John McEvoy, *Carlow College 1793-1993*. Carlow, Ireland: Carlovian Press, 1993. I identified alleged abusers among the Carlow priests from the BishopAccountability.org list of 2,000 priests accused of abuse in the United States. See www.BishopAccountability.org.

10. See Los Angeles archdiocese website, www.la-clergycases.com/library/addendum, November 15, 2005. In Portland, Oregon, the church's bankruptcy filing brought forth abuse accusations against 133 priests, more than three times the number reported earlier by the archdiocese. See Ashbel Green and Steve Woodward, "Claims in Court Far Outnumber Church Listing," *The Oregonian* (Portland, OR), November 12, 2006.

11. The author calculated this percentage by counting all those priests with Irish names among the 2,000 alleged abusers listed on BishopAccountability.org. The actual percentage would be higher because priests with Irish mothers and non-Irish fathers would not have an Irish name and could not be identified.

12. The gender of victims was obtained from various sources, mainly from newspaper articles cited in Google searches.

13. Los Angeles archdiocese website.

14. McEvoy, pp. 283-87

15. Telephone interview with Father Kevin Laheen, September 24, 2004

16. Telephone interview with Father Donal Gannon, November 1, 2004.

17. Los Angeles archdiocese website. Also see the legal complaint by Mia Lynn Giorgi in her lawsuit against Defendant Doe 1, et al. in State Superior Court in Los Angeles County, September 18, 2006.

18. "Diocese Denies Claim in Abuse Suit," Associated Press, February 27, 2005.

19. Internal memo in Catholic diocese of Yakima, WA, containing e-mail from Simpson victim, January 30, 2004.

20. E-mail from Kosnoff to the author, May 12, 2005.

21. E-mail from Kosnoff to the author, April 2, 2006.

22. McCaffrey, Lawrence J. *The Irish Catholic Diaspora in America*. Washington, D.C.: The Catholic University of America Press, 1997, pp.97-98.

23. Fuller, Louise. *Irish Catholicism Since 1950: The Undoing of a Culture*. Dublin: Gill & Macmillan, 2002, p. xxiv.

24. Smith, William L. "Irish Priests and American Catholicism: A Match Made in Heaven." *Social Scientific Study of Religion*, Vol. 9, JAI Press Inc., 1998

25. Moore, Chris. *Betrayal of Trust: The Father Brendan Smyth Affair and the Catholic Church*. Dublin: Marino Books, 1995, pp. 87, 205.

26. O'Grady deposition, p. 22. The Redemptorist religious order rejected him for physical and psychological reasons, so he went to St. Patrick's College seminary in Thurles, Ireland, from which he was ordained.

27. Kane, Gary. "Bishop Says Past 'Always Hung Over Me,'" *Palm Beach Post* (Palm Beach, FL), March 9, 2002. Documentation for O'Connell's history of sexual abuse will be cited in Chapter IV.

28. "All Hallows Pioneer Priests in the United States." Dublin: All Hallows College, p. 33.

29. John Jay College, p.41, for figures on American priests, and the author's calculations for figures on Irish priests, derived from various sources. Almost two-thirds of the American priests abused boys only while half of the Irish priests molested girls— including a small percentage who abused boys as well as girls. The author asserts that priests who abuse girls only or boys as well as girls are showing heterosexual behavior, while those who abuse only boys are showing homosexual behavior.

30. "Gary Crosby, Bing's Son and Actor," *New York Times*, August 26, 1995; "Philip Crosby, 69, Son of Bing Crosby," *New York Times*, January 20, 2004; Scott Haller and Maria Wilhelm, "The Sad Ballad of Bing and His Boys," online at http://community.mcckc.edu/crosby/bingboys.htm.

31. Smith, Irish Priests in the United States, p. 115.

32. Sipe, A. W. Richard. "Clergy Abuse in Ireland," *Wolves Within the Fold*. New Brunswick, NJ: Rutgers University Press, 1998, p. 146. The latest figures on Irish priests were supplied to the author by the Center for Applied Research in the Apostolate, Georgetown University, Washington, D.C.

33. "Bishop Is Accused of Sexual Abuse," *New York Times*, March 9, 2006.

34. The information on Renehan, Halford and Rister comes from e-mails to the author, a telephone interview with Renehan, newspaper articles, law-enforcement documents, and personal files of Rister.

35. "Women Say Ex-Pastor Sexually Abused Them," *Watertown Daily Times*, March 24, 2002. O'Doherty denied abusing them. Also see Mike McAndrew, "Two Women Sue Priest, Alleging Sex Abuse," *Post-Standard* (Syracuse, NY), March 23, 2002.

36. Complaint, A.B. as plaintiff, versus Bishop John Nevins of the Catholic Diocese of Venice et al, in Charlotte County Circuit Court, Florida, March 20, 1997.

37. Brumley, Jeff. "Diocese Settles Old Abuse Case," *Florida Times-Union* (Jacksonville, FL), Dec. 9, 2004.

38. O'Toole, Fintan. *The Lie of the Land*. London: Verso, 1997, p. 111

39. Internal memo in Catholic diocese of Yakima, WA.

CHAPTER THREE: CONSENTING ADULTS?

1. Engelhardt, Joel. "Priest Accused of Molesting Teen Girl, Groping Women," *Palm Beach Post*, April 19, 2002; personal diaries of the late Pat Hittel of Fort Lauderdale, FL. Engelhardt, "No Abuse Evidence on Priest, Police Say," *Palm Beach Post*, September 26, 2002. Flynn has denied some, but not all, of the accusations.

2. Parker, J. Michael. "Flores Disciplined Nine Priests, but Still Faces Some Criticism," *San Antonio Express-News*, April 28, 2002; Parker, "Officials Say Priest Sex Abuse Suit Settled to Ease Pain," *San Antonio Express-News*, February 22, 2003; Manny Gonzales, "Wayward Priest Dropped from Sex Abuse Lawsuit," *San Antonio Express-News*, February 19, 2003.

3. Letter from attorney Debra Talley to Archbishop Patrick Flores of San Antonio, Texas, September 9, 1993.

4. Hittel diaries and interviews with Bob Hittel in March 2005.

5. O'Connor, Lona. "Stolen Memories, Was Long 'Affair' Real or a Fantasy?" *Palm Beach Post*, December 12, 2004.

6. Engelhardt.

7. O'Connor, Lona. "Despite Diary, Former Priest Denies Affair," *Palm Beach Post*, December 12, 2004.

8. Engelhardt.

9. Ibid.

10. Interview with attorney Edward Ricci, February 24, 2004.

11. Ibid.

12. Engelhardt.

13. O'Connor.

14. "A Bishop Resigns," *New York Times*, June 7, 1998.

15. Perez-Reverte, Arturo. *Purity of Blood*. New York: Penguin, 1997, pp. 37-38.

16. Depositions of Father Michael Kenny for lawsuit, Julia Villegas Phelps v. Roman Catholic Archdiocese of San Antonio, Texas, and Kenny, in District Court of Bexar County. In the same lawsuit, see plaintiff's third amended complaint. Also see articles in *San Antonio Express-News*, cited above.

17. Ibid.

18. Ibid.

19. Letter from Archbishop Patrick Flores to woman claiming abuse by Father Paul Cleary, February 2, 1994.

20. Letter from woman to Flores describing the abuse and asking for help to pay for counseling, January 21, 1994.

21. Letter from Archbishop Flores to Dr. Maria T. Flores of the Marriage and Family Institute of San Antonio, July 5, 1994.

22. Letters from Catholic Mutual Group of San Antonio to officials of the San Antonio Catholic archdiocese, September 24, 1993, and March 3, 1994.

23. MacCormack, John. "Woman Claims She Took Fall for Priest," *San Antonio Express-News*, April 22, 2003; Guillermo Contreras, "Ex-Church Office Manager Gets 3+ Years for Theft," *San Antonio Express-News*, April 25, 2003.

24. Letter from Novak of Catholic Mutual Group.

25. "L[ong I[sland] Woman Reveals Priest Abuse," *Irish Voice*, June 1, 2004.

26. Catholic Mutual Group letters.

CHAPTER FOUR: THE BISHOP AND THE BOYS

1. Statement by Bishop Anthony J. O'Connell, *Palm Beach Post*, March 9, 2002.

2. Hobbs, Austin. "Clare Bishop in US Sex Scandal," *Clare Champion*, March 15, 2002.

3. These details of O'Connell's sexual involvements come from newspaper articles as well as court documents and attorney files in the five lawsuits filed by alleged victims.

4. Interview with Christopher Dixon, September 2, 2002.

5. Information on the three bishops comes from these sources: Interview of "Lindsay" by attorney Jeffrey Anderson, March 25, 2002; Kevin Kelly, "Miami, KC Papers Differ in Accounts of 'John Doe' Suit," *Catholic Key* (newspaper of the Diocese of Kansas City-

St. Joseph), April 26, 2002; Phillip O'Connor, "Coming to Terms, Confronting the Church," *Saint Louis Post-Dispatch*, November 15, 2004. For background, when a bishop is being considered for promotion, as was O'Connell, the Vatican embassy in Washington, D.C., routinely asks other bishops who know the candidate to report appropriate information, such as complaints of sexual abuse, that would bear on his candidacy. Although this process is carried out in secret, it can be assumed that McAuliffe, Gaydos, and Boland would have been among those asked about O'Connell. This is implicitly confirmed by Bishop Wilton Gregory calling it a "travesty" that church officials did not inform the Vatican of O'Connell's sexual abuse. See endnote 6 below.

6. "Gregory Calls Failure to Stop Appointment a 'Travesty.'" *National Catholic Reporter*, March 29, 2002.
7. Telephone interview with Flann Neylon, September 25, 2004.
8. Ireland Commission to Inquire into Child Abuse, Third Interim Report, December 2003, Dublin, Ireland, p. 170.
9. Breen, Pat. "From Lisheen to Tennessee," *Ballynacally-Lissycasey Parish Magazine*, November 15, 1988.
10. Ibid.
11. Interview with Father Frank O'Neill in Limerick, Ireland, September 16, 2004.
12. Telephone interviews with Fathers Gannon, Martin Igoe, and Joseph Brennan in late 2004.
13. E-mail from Fergus O'Donoghue, October 29, 2004.
14. O'Grady deposition.
15. John Jay College, p. 36.
16. Deposition of Bishop Anthony O'Connell, September 12, 2003, p. 54.
17. Lantigua, John. "Where a Fallen Bishop Goes to Heal," *Palm Beach Post*, April 18, 2004.
18. The National Review Board for the Protection of Children and Young People, "A Report on the Crisis in the Catholic Church in the United States," U.S. Conference of Catholic Bishops, February 27, 2004, p. 48.
19. Second amended complaint, John Doe Jr. vs. Bishop Anthony O'Connell et al, Circuit Court, Palm Beach County, FL, December 4, 2003.
20. Krauss, Clifford. "80,000 Native Canadians to Be Compensated for School Abuse," *New York Times*, April 27, 2006.
21. Information on the rape case against Father Robert Melancon comes from the criminal court file, State of Louisiana vs. Robert Melancon, Docket No. 264,226, Parish of Terrebonne, 1995-96, in Houma, LA.
22. Information on the Welsh case comes from many sources, including Report No. 86-54845 of the Spokane Police-Sheriff, September 30, 1986, as well as from police, church, and newspaper sources.

CHAPTER FIVE: Gay Boys

1. Deposition of Matthew Cosby, identified as John CC Doe, March 14, 2003, pp. 40-41.
2. Ibid, p. 147.
3. Ibid.

4. Congregation for Catholic Education.

5. Order and Judgment, David Darnold, senior circuit judge, John CC Doe vs. Anthony O'Connell et al, Circuit Court of Marion County, MO, January 9, 2004; Petition, John T Doe vs. O'Connell et al, Circuit Court of St. Louis County, MO, April 18, 2002; First Amended Petition, John Wm. Doe. vs. O'Connell et al, Marion County, April 11, 2002. Generally, the author uses the word "alleged" in describing unproved accusations. In this case he does not do so because O'Connell has admitted two of the sexual involvements; information on the others is found in lawsuits and depositions as well as a report by Phillip O'Connor in the *St. Louis Post- Dispatch* ("As scandal breaks, the search for truth begins," November 16, 2004). In addition, as noted, O'Connell pleaded the Fifth Amendment to avoid self-incrimination on all the allegations.

6. Documentation on the cover-up by the three bishops is found in Chapter 4, endnote 5.

7. O'Connor, Phillip. "Coming to Terms, Confronting the Church," *Saint Louis Post-Dispatch*, November 15, 2004. According to this account, based partly on a deposition, an O'Connell victim identified as "T. L." was kicked out of St. Thomas after he confided his sexual feelings about two younger students to O'Connell. The author has used the pseudonym "Tom Lindsay" for T. L because he has asked to remain anonymous to protect his privacy and that of his family.

8. The information in this paragraph comes from multiple sources as listed in note 5 above.

9. Deposition of Michael Wegs, August 5, 2003, p. 213.

10. Kane, Gary. "I Trusted Him with My Life, Victim Says." *Palm Beach Post*, March 15, 2002.

11. E-mail from "Tom Lindsay" to O'Connell, March 13, 2000.

12. E-mail from Lindsay to O'Connell, August 10, 2000.

13. O'Connor, Phillip. "Secret Sins and Silence," *Saint Louis Post Dispatch*, November 14, 2004. Information here also comes from the files of Lindsay's court case against O'Connell, in which he is identified as John T. Doe.

14. E-mail from O'Connell to Lindsay, March 15, 2000.

15. Judge Darnold, Order and Judgment.

16. Cosby deposition, pp. 30, 33, 35, 87; John CC Doe vs. O'Connell et al, plaintiff's opposition to motion for summary judgment, Circuit Court of Marion County, MO, March 1, 2004.

17. Ibid, p. 118.

18. Ibid, pp. 156-57.

19. O'Connor, and John T. Doe vs. O'Connell.

20. Ibid.

21. Ibid.

22. Driscoll, Amy. "Man Sues Ex-Palm Beach Bishop, Vatican." *Miami Herald*, April 19, 2002. Also see John CC Doe vs. O'Connell et al., p. 55.

23. The e-mails and notes come from the files of Lindsay's lawsuit against O'Connell.

24. Cosby deposition, pp. 124, 128-129.

25. Rice, Patricia. "Priest Ousted in Missouri Had Been Working at Disney World," *Saint Louis Post-Dispatch*, June 21, 2002.

26. An e-mail from Cosby to O'Connell, March 12, 2002, and an undated handwritten statement from the files of Cosby's lawsuit against O'Connell.

27. Kane, "I Trusted Him with My Life, Victim Says,"and Christine Stapleton, "Memories Won't Leave Him Alone," *Palm Beach Post*, March 9, 2002.
28. Lantiqua, John. "Accuser Decries Bishop's 'Plantation' Life," *Palm Beach Post*, May 17, 2004.
29. Wegs e-mail containing profile of O'Connell, sent to the author on December 3, 2003.
30. Wegs deposition, pp. 68-69, 102, 107, 109, 127, 136-137, 151.
31. O'Connor, "Coming to Terms, Confronting the Church."
32. O'Connor, Phillip. "As Scandal Breaks, Search for Truth Begins," *Saint Louis Post-Dispatch*, November 16, 2004.

CHAPTER SIX: THE IRISH SEEDBED

1. These headlines and stories are found on Thomas Crosbie Media (www.tcm.ie), October 25, 2005; *Irish Independent* (Dublin, Ireland), October 15, 2005; *Evening Echo* (Cork, Ireland), October 25, 2005.
2. *The Ferns Report*, presented to the Minister for Health and Children, Government of Ireland, October 2005.
3. O'Reilly, Emily. "Reporting the Catholic Church's Scandal in Ireland," *Nieman Reports*, Spring 2003.
4. O'Toole, Fintan. *The Lie of the Land*. London: Verso, 1997, p. 111.
5. Interview with Bishop William Walsh in Ennis, Ireland, September 22, 2004.
6. Half the Irish-born priests in America molested girls, according to the author's estimate, reported in Chapter 1 (p. 12 and endnote 3).
7. *Ferns Report*.
8. Ibid.
9. O'Connor, Alison. *A Message from Heaven*. Dingle, Ireland: Brandon, 2000, p. 7.
10. *Ferns Report*, pp. 31, 153-54.
11. "Bishops 'Ignored' Sexual Harassment of Student Priests," *Irish Times*, March 26, 2002; *Ferns Report*.
12. *Ferns Report*, p. 168.
13. Ibid., p. 148.
14. "102 Dublin Priests Suspected of Child Sex Abuse," *Toronto Star*, March 8, 2006.
15. Ibid.
16. Interview with Colm O'Gorman in Dublin, Ireland, September 15, 2004.
17. Interview with Mary Raftery, newspaper and television journalist, September 14, 2004, Dublin, Ireland.
18. Liebreich, Karen. *Fallen Order*. New York: Grove Press, 2004.
19. Raftery, Mary, and O'Sullivan, Eoin. *Suffer the Little Children: The Inside Story of Ireland's Industrial Schools*. Dublin: New Island Books, 2001, p. 254.
20. Interview with Brother Sean McNamara in Ennis, Ireland, September 9, 2004.
21. Interview with Father Patrick Conway in Ennis, Ireland, September 4, 2004.
22. Fahey, Tony, et al. Unpublished manuscript, the Economic and Social Research Institute, Dublin, 2004.

23. Wall, Martin. "Final Bill for Abuse in Care May Be 1.2 Billion [Euros]," *Irish Times*, October 13, 2006.
24. Cooney, John. "It's Time for the Purple Princes to Finally Fall on Their Croziers in Bid for Credibility," *Irish Independent* (Dublin), November 1, 2005.
25. Hoban, Brendan. *Change or Decay: Irish Catholicism in Crisis*. Dublin: Banley House, 2005. Hoban is a parish priest.
26. Cahill; Richard Killeen. *A Short History of Ireland*. Dublin: Gill & Macmillan, 1994.
27. Laxton, Edward. *Famine Ships: The Irish Exodus to America*. New York: Henry Holt and Company, 1998.

CHAPTER SEVEN: CELIBACY AND SEX

1. *Ferns Report*, p. 18.
2. Goode, p.10.
3. Finkelhor, David. "Child Sexual Abuse: Reflections on the Irish Profile," Director, Crimes Against Children Research Center, University of New Hampshire, Durham, NH.
4. Hanson, R. Karl, et al. *Sexual Abuse in the Catholic Church: Scientific and Legal Perspectives*. Proceedings of the conference "Abuse of Children and Young People by Catholic Priests and Religious," Pontifical Academy for Life, Vatican City, April 2-5, 2003.
5. Raftery interview.
6. Ranke-Heinemann, Uta. *Eunuchs for the Kingdom of Heaven*. New York: Doubleday, 1990, p. 325.
7. Flannery interview.
8. O'Grady deposition.
9. Dezell, Maureen, *Irish America: Coming into Clover*. New York: Anchor Books, 2002, p. 121.
10. Hanson, pp. 33-34.
11. Letters involving Father Michael Simpson, diocese of Yakima, WA, February 18, 1972, through January 21, 1977.
12. Grimes, William. "Twisting Along China's Sharp Curves," *New York Times*, August 4, 2006.
13. Leader interview.
14. Interview with Father Hugh Behan, March 19, 2005.
15. Cornwell, John. *Seminary Boy*. New York: Doubleday, 2006. This information is scattered throughout the book.
16. Hanson, p. 147.
17. O'Reilly interview.
18. Interview with Brother Sean McNamara in Ennis, Ireland, September 9, 2004.
19. Berry, Jason and Gerald Renner. *Vows of Silence*. New York: Free Press, 2004, p. 71.
20. France, David. *Our Fathers: The Secret Life of the Catholic Church in an Age of Scandal*. New York: Broadway Books, 2004, pp. 197,199; William Lobdell, "Priest Who Admitted to Sex Abuse of Teen Agrees to Leave the Clergy," *Los Angeles Times*, March 29, 2002.

21. Wegs profile of Anthony O'Connell.

22. Thavis, John. "Vatican: Church Must Work with Scientific Experts to Prevent Abuse," *Catholic News Service*, February 18, 2004.

23. *Ferns Report*, p. 36.

24. Conway, Eamonn. "Making a Good Confession: Acknowledging Cultural and Structural Issues in the Child Sexual Abuse Crisis in the Roman Catholic Church." Mary Immaculate College, University of Limerick, Limerick, Ireland, September 2004.

25. "Hello Boys," *Sunday Independent Life*, September 19, 2004.

26. "Will She Go the Distance?" *Sunday Times Style*, September 12, 2004.

27. O'Toole, Fintan. "The Demons Within," *Irish Times*, September 27, 2004.

28. "Let's Talk about Sex," *Independent Life*, September 28, 2004.

29. Humphreys, Joe. "Over Half of Limerick Births Outside Marriage," *Irish Times*, September 30, 2004.

30. Kenny, Mary. "The Last Fanfare of Good Old Catholic Ireland," *Sunday Independent*, September 26, 2004.

31. Lavery, Brian. "Scandal? For an Irish Parish, It's Just a Priest with a Child," *New York Times*, January 22, 2006.

32. Cahill, pp. 135, 138.

33. Durant, Will. *The Age of Faith*. New York: Simon and Schuster, 1950, p. 82.

34. O'Sullivan, Timothy. "The 'New' Irish," Office of Migration & Refugee Services, U.S. Conference of Catholic Bishops, June 3, 2003.

35. O'Toole, "The Demons Within," p. 75.

36. Miller, Kerby. *Emigrants and Exiles*. New York: Oxford University Press, 1985, pp. 280, 404.

37. McCaffrey, p. 82.

38. Miller, pp. 403–04; McCaffrey, p. 82.

39. Goode, p. 32.

40. Sipe, "Clergy Abuse in Ireland," p. 149.

41. McCaffrey, p. 81.

42. Ibid, p. 82, and interview with James Smith of Irish Studies at Boston College, July 26, 2004.

43. Ranke-Heinemann, p. 267.

44. Dolan, J. P., historian, University of Notre Dame, interviewed by the editors of *U.S. Catholic*, March 10, 2004.

45. Fuller, Louise. *Irish Catholicism Since 1950: The Undoing of a Culture*. Dublin: Gill & Macmillan, 2002, p. 253.

46. O'Toole, "The Demons Within," p. 74.

47. Hoban, Brendan. *Change or Decay: Irish Catholicism in Crisis*. Dublin: Banley House, 2005

CHAPTER EIGHT: THE POPE AND IRELAND

1. Keenan, Paul. "Ireland Remembers 'Three Wonderful Days,'" *Irish Catholic*, September 23, 2004.

2. McGarry, Patsy. "Rape of Boy during Papal Visit Recalled," *Irish Times*, September 10, 2004.

3. O'Toole, *The Lie of the Land*, pp. 76-78, 109, 117; James Smith and Robert Savage, "Sexual Abuse and the Irish Church: Crisis and Responses," Occasional Paper #8, Irish Studies Program, Boston College, Boston, MA, April 15, 2003.

4. Cornwell, John. *Breaking Faith*. New York: Penguin Putnam Inc., 2001, p. 241-42.

5. Inglis, Tom. *Moral Monopoly: The Catholic Church in Modern Irish Society*. Dublin: Gill & Macmillan, 1987, p. 207.

6. Interview with Father Raphael Gallagher of Alfonsiana Academy in Rome, October 31, 2001.

7. Josef Votzi interview with Josef Hartmann, *Profil*, March 27, 1995. Also, "Austria: Facing Allegations, Cardinal Retires," *Christianity Today*, October 2, 1995.

8. Letter to the Bishops of Austria from Pope John Paul II, September 8, 1995.

9. "Already in 1985 Father Udo Fischer Demanded of Groer's Superiors to Investigate Relevant Allegations," *Profil*, April 2, 1995.

10. "Why the Abbot Acted," *Dialog*, February 1998.

11. Donovan, Gill. "Cardinal Hans Herman Groer Resigned Over Sex Abuse," *National Catholic Reporter*, April 11, 2003.

12. Interview with Vatican journalist Marco Politi, November 15, 2001.

13. This information comes from a confidential source formerly in the Gemelli Clinic.

14. Bishop Moore's death certificate, from the Minnesota Department of Health. Also, Joe Sexton, "Death of a Bishop: Of Holy Orders and Human Frailty," *New York Times*, October 7, 1995.

15. Marinelli, Msgr. Luigi, et al. *Shroud of Secrecy*. Toronto: Key Porter Books, Ltd., 2000.

16. Stanley, Alessandra. "Tell-All Book Creates Furor at Vatican," *New York Times*, July 17, 1999.

17. Interview with Giovanni Avenna of the Adista Catholic News Agency, October 17, 2001, and e-mail from Marjan Agerbeek, Dutch journalist, January 19, 2002.

18. Letters to author from Italian bishop accused of sex abuse, one undated and the other November 15, 2002.

19. Allen Jr., John L. "Polish Prelate Accused of Sexual Abuse," *National Catholic Reporter*, March 16, 2002.

20. Kaiser, Robert Blair, *Rome Diary 43*, sent on-line April 1, 2002.

21. Letter to the author from Msgr. Denis O'Callaghan, vicar general for Bishop John Magee in the Diocese of Cloyne, Ireland, October 29, 2002.

22. Telephone interview with Irish journalist Sam Smyth, March 2003. For Magee's role in the 1981 strike, see Peter Beresford, *Ten Men Dead* (London: HarperCollins Publishers Ltd., 1987), chapter 3. According to this account, the Brits were hostile to Magee's attempt on behalf of the pope to settle the strike. After failing in his mission, Magee issued a statement assuring that the pope would continue seeking ways to help the people of Ireland work out solutions to their communal problems in accord with Christian teaching, a statement not calculated to win favor in Protestant Britain.

23. Berry, Jason. "Second-Guessing John Paul II," *Los Angeles Times*, May 28, 2006. For a definitive account of this case, see the book *Vows of Silence* by Berry and Gerald Renner (New York: Free Press, 2004).

24. Telephone interview with Cardinal William Wakefield Baum in Washington, D.C., January, 10, 2003.

25. Penouel, Stephan. "Swiss Guard and Gay," *Panorama*, February 15, 2001.

26. Interview in Rome with Vladimir Luxuria, November 7, 2001.

27. Interview in Rome with Sister Marie McDonald of the Missionaries of Our Lady of Africa, November 17, 2001.

28. "Changes in Episcopate," *L'Osservatore Romano*, October 3, 2001.

29. Kaiser, Robert Blair. *A Church in Search of Itself.* New York: Alfred A. Knopf, 2006, p. 222.

30. Thavis, John. "Vatican Spokesman Say Sex Abuse Raises Questions About U.S. Morals," *Catholic News Service*, June 23, 1993.

31. Economus, Tom. "The Controversial Pope," The Link Up (http://www.healingall.org), August 3, 2001.

32. Sipe, p. 142, and the *Ferns Report*.

33. O'Toole, p. 76.

34. "Papal Message to the Irish Bishops," Irish School of Evangelisation, June 26, 1999.

35. Flannery, "Abuse Victims Need to Try to Let Go," Redemptorist Publications Online, February 2004.

36. O'Doherty, Caroline, and Michael Brennan. "Irish Bishop Speaks out on a Married Priesthood," *Irish Examiner*, from Thomas Crosbie Media (www.tcm.ie), 2005.

37. De Rosa, Peter. *Vicars of Christ*. New York: Crown Publishers, 1988. See chapter 20, "Unchaste Celibates," for an account of the history of celibacy.

38. Wills, Garry. *Papal Sin*. New York: Doubleday, 2000, p.123.

39. For information on the Ronan case see John V. Doe vs. Holy See et al, opinion and order, U.S. District Judge Michael Mosman, June 7, 2006; John V. Doe, amended complaint, March 31, 2004; "Oregon Loses Bid for Immunity in Oregon Clergy Abuse Lawsuit," Jurist website (http://jurist.law.pitt.edu), June 8, 2006.

40. "Kentucky Judge Allows Sex Abuse Lawsuit against Vatican to Go Forward," *USA Today*, January 11, 2007.

41. Meichtry, Stacy. "Pope Urges Poles to Help Revive Europe's Churches," *Religion News Service*, May 2006.

42. Address of Pope Benedict XVI to the Irish Bishops, October 28, 2006, press release from the Catholic Communications Office of the Irish Bishops' Conference.

CHAPTER NINE: SHARED SECRETS

1. Peet, Judy. "Church abuse settlement dismays priest's supporters," *Newark Star-Ledger* (Newark, NJ), February 2, 2002.

2. McGreevey, James. *The Confession*. New York: Regan, HarperCollins, 2006, p. 326.

3. Bootkoski, Bishop Paul, diocese of Metuchen, letter to members of St. James parish, September 2, 2003.

4. Carroll, Dore, and Brian Murray. "N[ew] J[ersey] Diocese Settles Sex Abuse Claim," *Newark-Star Ledger*, January 30, 2003.
5. McGreevey, p. 95.
6. Ibid., p. 183.
7. Ibid., p. 334.
8. Ibid., p. 62.
9. Doyle, Thomas P., Sipe, and Patrick J. Wall, *Sex Priests, and Secret Codes*. Los Angeles: Volt Press, 2006, p. 295. Doyle, a Dominican priest, is one of the world's foremost experts on clergy sex abuse, having testified in hundreds of cases. Wall is a former priest and senior consultant on sex abuse cases at the Manly & McGuire law firm. I gave Sipe's background above in the text.
10. Ibid., p. 12.
11. Ibid., p. x.
12. Sipe, *A Secret World*, p. 47.
13. De Rosa, p. 405.
14. Ibid.
15. Ibid.
16. Greeley, Andrew. *Furthermore! Memories of a Parish Priest*. New York: Tom Doherty Associates, 1999, p. 77.
17. Information for this section on Michael Kenny comes from depositions, medical records and other documents from a lawsuit brought by Julia Villegas Phelps against Kenny and the archdiocese of San Antonio, TX, in the District Court of Bexar County.
18. Burkett, Elinor, and Frank Bruni. *A Gospel of Shame*. New York: Penguin Books, 1993, p. 50.
19. Cozzens, Donald. *The Changing Face of the Priesthood*. Collegeville, MN: The Liturgical Press, 2000, p.119.
20. The Congregation for Catholic Education.
21. Allen, John L. Jr., "The Word from Rome," *National Catholic Reporter*, Dec. 2, 2005.

CHAPTER TEN: AN EPILOGUE AND MORE

1. The information for this section of the epilogue comes from the files of the Palm Beach County State Attorney, the prosecutor in the theft case against the two priests. Included are investigative reports of the Delray Beach Police Department, and sworn testimony, under questioning, of church employees Renee Wardrip, Terese Roehm Duffey, and Colleen Duffey Head.
2. This section of the epilogue is based primarily on a motion to compel Bishop Robert Brom to testify and produce documents regarding allegations of sexual misconduct against him, February 19, 2007, and a deposition of Brom, November 30–December 1, 2006, both in San Diego Superior Court, California. The proceedings are part of the sexual abuse case titled, Clergy Cases II, John B., plaintiff, versus John Doe I, et al, defendants, also in San Diego Superior Court.

INDEX

A REQUEST FOR INFORMATION

Author Joe Rigert is continuing his research on sex abuse in the Catholic church, now focusing again on the sexual involvements of bishops. He would appreciate receiving from readers any new information they might have on this matter. Please e-mail him at Rigertetc@aol.com.

1423516

Made in the USA